The shapes, patterns and textures of reinforced concrete structures such as the staircase and the water tower are the result of the efficient use of this material. The houses of the modern Spanish village are designed in a modern idiom but are built of traditional materials and by traditional methods. They will fit into the landscape for which they were designed.

The plastic handle of a saw is designed to be efficient in use. Its amazing subtlety is due to the fact that the designer has fully understood its purpose and thoroughly experienced its form. The same is true of the poker at the left.

12   BAKER

Looking and Seeing 1

PATTERN AND SHAPE

by Kurt Rowland MSIA

Ginn and Company Ltd.
18 Bedford Row
London WC1

About this book

The object of the four parts *Looking and Seeing* is to encourage the rising generation to examine the shapes and patterns which form the background of human life. The author believes that such an experience will provide them with standards of value which may be applied to everything they see.

There was a time when all man-made things were produced by craftsmen who understood the materials they used and the shapes they created. Their methods of working were changed to meet changing conditions and, steadily improving, were passed on from one generation to the next. This living tradition was shattered by the Industrial Revolution, when handicraft was replaced by powerful forces which no one seemed able to control effectively. The buildings in which people lived and worked and the objects they used in daily life broke with the past and assumed totally new shapes. At the same time large numbers of mechanical devices were invented, so that man's environment was changed and distorted to an extent quite unprecedented.

We have now passed through what some people regard as the First Machine Age, and we are about to reap the benefits brought by science and technology. We have learnt to exert a certain amount of control over our world, over our surroundings and the lives we lead within them. But although we have gained much we have probably lost even more. We no longer possess the knowledge and the understanding to judge the things we make: our houses and factories, our implements and machines, our cities and roads. Because of this failure in judgement, we often find ourselves surrounded with such ugliness as would have horrified men of past ages.

The next period in our history may well be one of construction and technical progress, but all this great creative effort will be of little value to us if we cannot learn to control the shapes and patterns which form the background of our lives. It is now more important than ever that we should learn to understand the basic laws of the world around us, the man-made world and the world of nature, for the visual impact of our surroundings has a deep and lasting effect on us all.

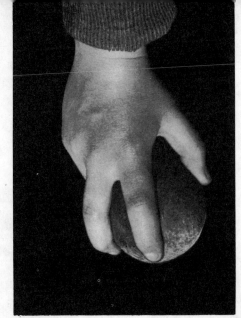

Contents

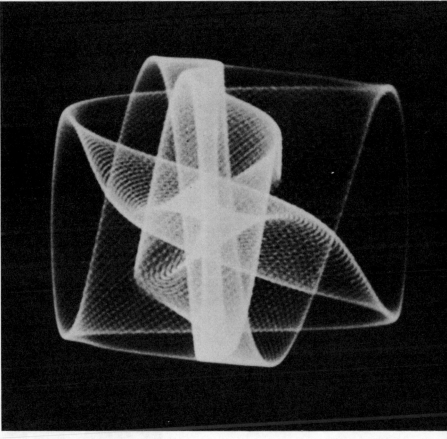

© K F Rowland 1964
Third impression 1965
156505
Printed in Great Britain
by W S Cowell Ltd
at the Butter Market, Ipswich

The author wishes to offer his especial thanks to the many people who have helped him in his search for illustrations. Full acknowledgements to copyright holders and exact details of sources are to be found in the Teachers' Book which accompanies the series.

3

I

2

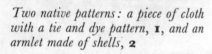

3

4

*Two native patterns: a piece of cloth with a tie and dye pattern, **1**, and an armlet made of shells, **2***

3. *A Greek sculptured head with highly patterned hair and beard*

4. *One of the many patterns which can be produced in expanded metal*

Thinking about patterns

What does the word 'pattern' mean to you? What do you think of when you hear it or read it? To most people it means simply a design in which a certain thing is repeated many times.

A pattern may be no more than a potato cut repeated until it covers a certain area, **5**, or it may be a piece of expanded metal. If you look at objects made hundreds or even thousands of years ago you will find patterns on them, although many of these patterns will be different from the patterns of our own day. The patterns of less civilised people and those of different cultures also differ from our own. But the patterns you can see on these pages have one thing in common:

5

they are highly suitable for the materials with which or on which they were made. This is one of the most important qualities to look for in any pattern.

6

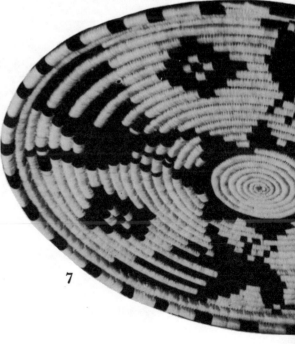

7

Patterns of stone, **6**, *and basketwork,* **7**

Part of the wall of the nunnery, Chichen Itza, Mexico

The pattern of the wall of this nunnery in Mexico, **1**, took shape while the wall was being built, and is part of the wall itself. The pattern on the pottery lamp base, **2**, is also part of the object itself. It was produced by scratching lines into the clay before glazing. The pattern on the tweed, **3**, is typical of the kind of pattern which can be woven into this fabric. If you wanted to remove any of these patterns you would have to destroy the objects on which you find them. As we shall see, patterns which are closely linked to their surfaces are usually the best patterns. Our surroundings often provide us with ideas for patterns. The pattern on the wallpaper, **5**, may have been inspired by the sight of a park in autumn, when lawns and paths are strewn with leaves. A printer's type case may have given someone the idea of making tiles decorated with letters, and the pattern which comes about when such tiles are placed side by side, **6**, can be very interesting.

2 3

4 5

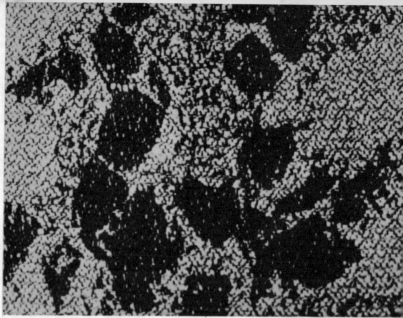

1

Although our surroundings may give us the basic shapes for our patterns, these shapes often change during the process of pattern-making and are difficult to recognise when the pattern is finished. The fabric pattern, **2**, was produced from a detail, **1**, taken from a very much larger photograph of leaves. In the same way a photograph of sun-dried, cracked mud, **3**, provided a pattern for a carpet, **4**.

3

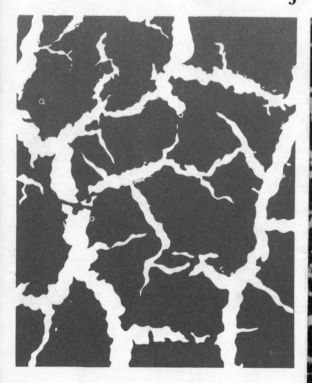

5   6

Pictures **5** to **8** show how a photograph of a wall turns into a pattern on a fabric. A part of the photograph is enlarged and reduced to black and white, **5**, **6**. This black-and-white design is then repeated, **7**, **8**. The finished pattern looks just right, but this does not come about by accident. If the pattern had been treated differently, constructed differently, used on different cloth, printed in different colours, it might have been a failure.

The patterns shown in pictures **2**, **4**, **7**, **8** are taken from the surroundings of the people who made them. They show that you can find patterns in the most unlikely places if you will only look for them. Yet fabrics with patterns like these would have been quite impossible not so many years ago. Why is this?

7   8

1

Picture **1** shows a nineteenth-century pattern and you can see that it is quite unlike most patterns of the present day. Everything in it is neat and careful. Many nineteenth-century patterns look rather like this one. We can describe them as *formal*. Life itself was formal, too. There were rules for what to wear and what to say in company, how to curtsey, what to write in a letter, what to eat and drink at certain times, and so on. Even a picnic could be a formal affair. Nowadays we live differently; we are much freer and have fewer rules to tie us down. We can do all kinds of things which in the past were forbidden. Because of this we are free to look for patterns where we like, even in dried-up river beds.

2   3

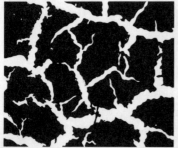

5 **6**

Look out of the window and you will probably see a building on which is a pattern of brickwork. If it is a large building, with many windows, these too will form themselves into a pattern. If you live in a street of small houses and you look down the street, then the houses themselves will link up into a pattern. The flagstones of the pavement will be laid in a definite pattern and there may be a fence or an iron gate to add still more patterns. If you take the trouble to look at things carefully, you will find patterns everywhere. You will find them in the most unexpected places, and will discover them even in familiar objects where you have not noticed them before.

7

8 **9**

1

You may think of patterns as being regular and repeated evenly, but you never in fact see a pattern in that way. Imagine you are standing on a large open space which is paved with rectangular slabs. All the slabs are square and the men who laid them have taken great pains to make sure they are all in line. Seen from an aeroplane the slabs will look square and the passengers will say how beautifully even the pattern is. But from your viewpoint as you stand on the ground the pattern looks as it does in picture 1. The change in the appearance of the pattern is called *distortion*. You cannot find two slabs which are the same shape. You can, however, feel the slabs as a pattern and you would not dream of complaining that they get smaller the farther away from you they are. This unevenness or distortion is sometimes an advantage. Compare what the passengers in the aircraft can see of the pattern with your own view. Don't you think that your pattern is much more interesting to look at? What applies to the paved floor also applies to most of the patterns you look at, wallpapers and carpets for example. You may not always think of it, but the part of a pattern farther away from you, even only a few inches away, must look smaller than the part close to you. This distortion is greater where the pattern is not on a flat surface. Patterns are often put on to porcelain and pottery by means of transfers, much like the picture transfers you may have played with. Picture 3 shows how such transfers look when printed flat. Picture 2 shows the same transfer used on pottery.

2 3

Patterns on soft materials such as paper and fabrics may become even more distorted. About half the pattern in picture **4** is hidden by the folds and broken up. Nevertheless, anyone looking at it recognises it as a pattern in spite of the breaks and distortion. Pattern is something that is felt rather than thought about. What is the difference between pictures **5** and **6**? One is made up of unrelated shapes, the other of shapes which are similar. Neither has a repeating pattern in it, yet one does not look like a pattern and the other does. Why? Remember these two pictures—we shall come back to them later.

4

5 6

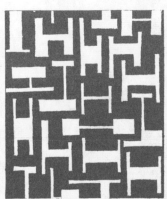

7 8

*The patterns in **7** and **8** are either distorted or irregular, or broken up by other patterns—yet we can feel them as patterns.*

1

TO SUM UP

Pattern-making is and always has been an important human activity and we live surrounded by patterns. They have something to do with the materials of which they are made, or with the surfaces on which they appear, or with the surroundings of their makers, or all of these. Pattern is something you sense when you see it, even if it is irregular and there is no exact repetition.

EXERCISES

1. Find three repeating patterns in your home or in school and three more out of doors. Draw them.
2. Find three examples of patterns which we often see in a distorted state, and make drawings of them.
3. Do you think that cracks in mud are natural patterns like flowers? What have such patterns in common? Give examples of other natural patterns.
4. Do you think the pattern of the paved floor becomes more interesting when it is distorted? Why do you think so?
5. The Greek artist who decorated this vase, **1**, did not use a transfer but painted the decoration straight onto the vase. Which method do you think is better?
6. Pictures **2** to **5** show patterns which do not repeat exactly. Find three patterns in your house similar to these, and three more out of doors. Make rough sketches of them.

2

3

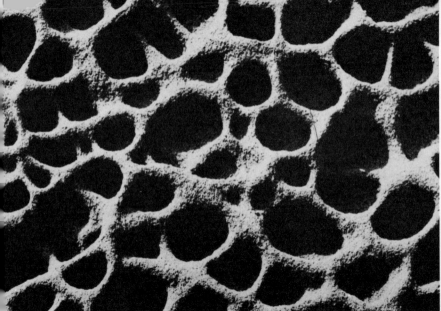

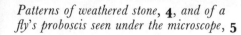

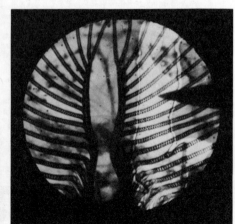

2

Patterns are caused by materials

In the last chapter we looked at all kinds of patterns which were thought of by artists, designers and architects, and made either by hand or by machine. Let us call them man-made patterns. We also looked at natural patterns, formed by flowers or leaves or water. Man-made patterns, of which we find many in our surroundings, are a very important part of human life. From the earliest days of man's history, he has decorated fabrics, pottery vessels, tools, buildings— indeed most of the things he uses.

We must not think of pattern as something which comes with refinement and luxury only after a high state of civilisation has been reached. The earliest, crudest things made by man were often decorated with patterns. It may seem that any time spent on pattern making is wasted, because a pattern does not add to the usefulness of the fabric or vessel which it decorates, and that this time would be better employed in trying to make a stronger fabric or vessel. Is this in fact so? When one looks at very old objects, the pattern seems to be part of the object. One feels that this earthenware vessel, **1**, and the pattern on it belong together, that one could not exist without the other. This may seem strange, but it will be easier to understand if you try to discover how the earliest patterns developed.

1

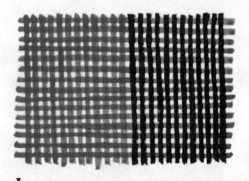

How did the idea of pattern first come to early man? Perhaps one day he was weaving a length of cloth and his supply of thread gave out. The only other thread he had was of a different kind or colour and rather than leave his cloth unfinished he made do with that. He may have been pleased with the effect which came about through the use of contrasting threads and for his next piece of weaving perhaps he chose such threads intentionally. As time went by he became more and more skilled, and could produce many different patterns.

I

2

2. Spinners and weavers in ancient Greece, about 560 B.C.

Before the potter's wheel was invented clay vessels were built up of long strips of soft clay. To prevent such a vessel from sagging and losing its shape whilst drying a rope was wound round it to hold it together, **3**. The rope often produced a ring-like decoration on the surface of the vessel, **4**, and it is easy to imagine that this pattern may have pleased the early potters. The users of the vessel may have been pleased, too, especially when they found that the markings made the pot much easier to grasp and lift up. On early pieces of pottery, fluted decorations, **5**, made with the fingers while the clay was still wet, also served to provide a grip.

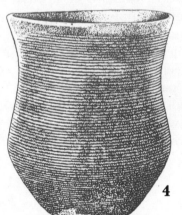

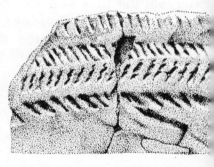

3

4   5

6

7

Or let us think of a later potter, who has just finished his first vessel on his brand new potter's wheel. When our potter proudly looked at his vessel, he may have noticed a few unevennesses; his fingers, as they moulded the clay, might have left one or two rings marked on the surface, **6**. Perhaps he liked the pattern made in this way and when he next made a vessel he may have purposely put in the ring marks, which before had been just an accident. Later he found that if he held the point of a sharp tool against the side of the vessel as it turned on the wheel he could make the pattern of rings even more pronounced, **7**.

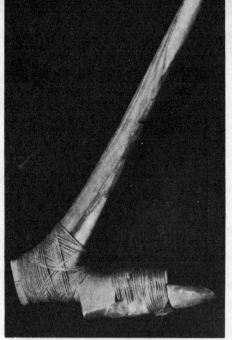

1 2

An early toolmaker might have been trying to find the best way of binding the blade of an axe to its shaft with string, when he found that he could make an efficient joint in the way shown in pictures **1** and **2**. This joint is not only neat and practical but it makes a pattern which must have pleased the early toolmaker for he developed it in many different ways.

You will have noticed that all the patterns we have discussed so far in this chapter have something to do with the objects on which they appear. They are closely related either to the purpose of the object or to the material of which it is made. Long ago when man found it very difficult to make things, he had to understand his materials really well to get the best results from them. He could not have produced all the wonderful things we see in museums without a deep understanding of such materials as metal, stone, wood, leather and woven fabrics. He seems to have realised the special qualities of each material, suited to certain purposes and useless for others.

Because he understood his materials, early man was able to make beautiful things, using only the simplest tools. In the same way, modern craftsmen, with an understanding of the potentialities and limitations of their materials, are able to make beautiful objects like those shown opposite, **4** to **7**.

*The pattern of this Persian glass bottle, **3**, was produced by the same process as the bottle. Because of this the pattern is suitable not only to the material but to the shape of the bottle itself.*

3

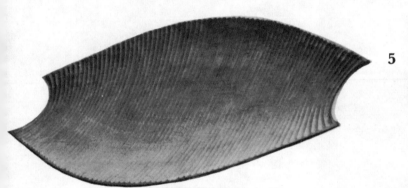

4

5

6 7

All these modern objects were produced by people who are masters of their craft. The woven pattern, **4**, and the pottery pattern, **7**, could only have been produced by craftsmen who knew how their materials would behave. The wooden bowl, **5**, has the actual tool marks for a pattern. The Swedish wooden cross, **6**, makes use of the curl of the wood when it is cut in a certain way.

*The pattern of the ancient bronze mirror, **1**, and the modern pottery bowl, **2**, although thousands of years apart, show the same respect for their materials; but could one say the same of patterns **4** to **8**?*

3

Nowadays we find it much easier to make things, for we have the help of machines. The person who works a machine seldom needs to know much about his material; the machine has made this unnecessary. Good patterns spring from an understanding of the materials they are used on. Because many of us have lost this understanding our patterns are often very

much worse than those of early craftsmen.

Pictures **4** to **8** show a number of patterns produced in our own time. Can you see that they do not grow from their materials and in fact do not seem to belong to them?

Now look again at the examples of modern patterns on page 19. Can you sense in these a kind of friendship between pattern and material? The reason for the difference between the good modern patterns on page 19 and those shown here is that the people who made the objects on this page had no real understanding of the material they were using. Perhaps the men who designed the patterns did not even know how the objects were to be made.

4

6

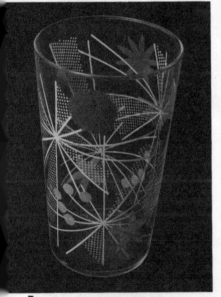

5

7

8

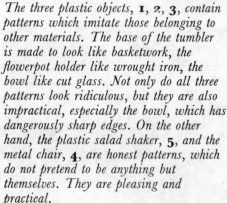

*The three plastic objects, **1**, **2**, **3**, contain patterns which imitate those belonging to other materials. The base of the tumbler is made to look like basketwork, the flowerpot holder like wrought iron, the bowl like cut glass. Not only do all three patterns look ridiculous, but they are also impractical, especially the bowl, which has dangerously sharp edges. On the other hand, the plastic salad shaker, **5**, and the metal chair, **4**, are honest patterns, which do not pretend to be anything but themselves. They are pleasing and practical.*

In recent years new materials and new processes have been invented. The people who work with these new materials need new patterns to match them. Pictures **1** to **3** show how ugly objects can be when we decorate them by imitating old patterns, unsuited to the new materials. Look by contrast at pictures **4** to **9** and you will recognise good modern patterns, which have grown from new materials.

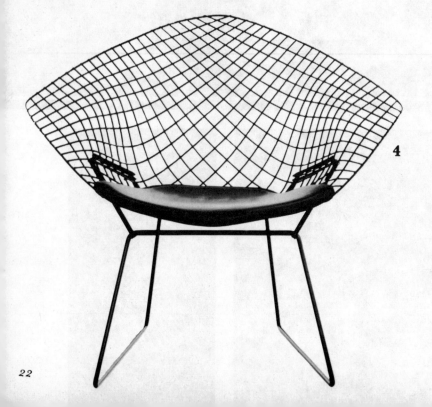

4

5

6. *Exhibition Hall in Turin.* 8. *The smaller Sports Palace in Rome. Both in reinforced concrete, designed by Nervi.*
7. *Model of a tower made of glass and steel, to be used for exhibitions.* 9. *Pottery tiles, made by a new process, which can be used for large open work screens. All these patterns make the best use of modern materials and methods, which accounts for their attractiveness.*

6

7

1

2

*The pattern on this pottery tile, **1**, is taken from a woodcut, **2**. Notice how glazing and firing have changed the design.*

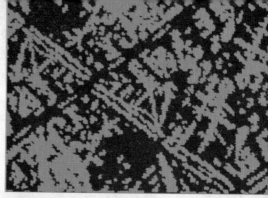

3

4

It is possible to use the same basic design for different materials if it is done by someone who understands them. Pictures **3**, **4** and **6** show how a single design can be used on different materials. Because the materials and processes are different the final patterns also vary. In each case the pattern has been adapted to the material with skill and imagination.

TO SUM UP

Good patterns are born from man's understanding of materials such as wood, fabrics, clay, glass, or stone. There must be friendship between pattern and material. To make a good pattern you must know a lot about the material. New materials need new patterns to fit them.

EXERCISES

1. Compare the Greeks weaving a pattern on page 16 with the man printing a pattern on page 20. What is one important difference between the two operations? What do you think the attitude of each worker will be to his pattern?

2. Find some patterns which you think are suited to the material on which they are used. Make drawings of them and explain why they are suitable. Do the same with patterns which are unsuitable for their material.

3. Do you find anything wrong with the patterns in pictures **8** and **9**?

*Madonna and child in stone, **5**, and draped reclining figure in bronze, **7**, both by Henry Moore*

5

*Both the carpet, **3**, and the woven fabric, **4**, were derived from the same basic pattern, **6**. Because the materials and processes are different the final patterns also vary.*

6

*The outer cases of these vacuum flasks, **8** and **9**, are made of metal; the patterns are printed.*

4. Why did people make fewer bad patterns in the past?

5. The two statues, **5** and **7**, were made by the same sculptor. Compare the two patterns of folds in the drapery, remembering that the statues were made by different processes.

8

9

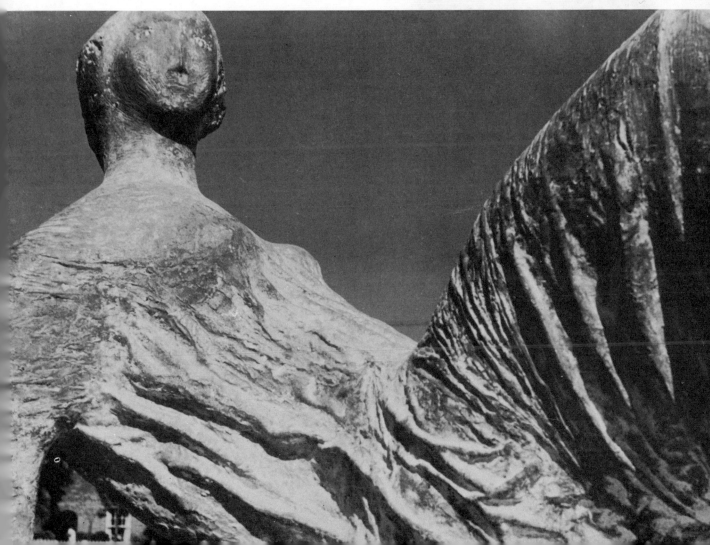

Patterns from our surroundings

3

Although patterns are sometimes made up of lines and shapes which we cannot recognise as definite objects, they more often contain shapes which we know quite well: leaves, flowers, birds, even mud-cracks.
Plant forms are the most commonly used shapes for patterns because they lend themselves so well to pattern-making; they grow in a pattern-like way. There are numberless ways of making patterns from a plant shape. Picture **1** shows a Greek stone carving derived from the strong natural shape of the vine which occurs in many Greek patterns. The acanthus

1

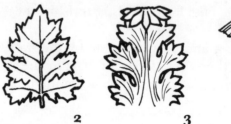

2   3   4

leaf was another favourite subject with the Greeks. Pictures **2** to **4** show how they changed this to fit their patterns, but it is still recognisable. The fleur-de-lis, **5**, is familiar in French patterns. This shape was originally used in the arms of the kings of France. It looks somewhat different from the Madonna lily on which it is based, although the flower can still be recognised. Picture **6** shows a very simple pattern using the fleur-de-lis. Oak leaves often appear in English patterns, as you can see in this carved capital from Southwell Minster, **7**.

5

6

7

The Eskimos often use animal shapes in their patterns. Picture **8** shows a hunting tool on which the owner has carved a pattern of reindeer.

8

The Greek vine and acanthus, the French lily, the English oak, the Eskimo reindeer: what have all these in common? The acanthus and the vine are common sights in Greece, where even the humblest peasant grows grapes and makes his own wine. The lily thrives in France. The English landscape is unthinkable without the oak. The Eskimo rarely sees any trees or flowers, but the reindeer is familiar to him. Picture **8** shows how well the carver observed and understood these animals. What is it then that all these natural shapes have in common?

9

Men create patterns from things they see around them. You cannot make a pattern from something unless you are very familiar with it. Making a pattern requires skill. The pattern-maker must often modify the shapes of flowers or animals to fit his purpose. To do this he must know a great deal about those plants or animals. A poem is also a pattern, a pattern of words. In a poem the words have to be arranged until they fall into a certain pattern which the poet wants. Often the words are slightly changed, just as flower shapes may be changed in order to fit into a pattern. Have you ever tried to write a poem? If so, you will appreciate that in order to write a good poem the poet must know a great deal about the words he uses. In the same way, no one can construct a good pattern without understanding the shapes he is using. And what shapes do we know better than the shapes around us, amongst which we have grown up? That is why people use familiar objects for their patterns. But surroundings are not the same in all parts of the world, and as the surroundings change, so the patterns change: the Greek vine and acanthus; the French lily, the English oak, the Eskimo reindeer. In their own countries these are common: the oak leaf is quite ordinary to us. But what is common in one place

10

11

12

is unusual in another. Our oak leaves would look just as unusual to the Eskimo as his reindeer do to us. Although patterns may be different because they are made in different surroundings, their makers have one thing in common: they share an understanding of what is meant by pattern. Men may live in different parts of the world, they may have different customs, their skins may be of different colours, but their minds work in very similar ways.

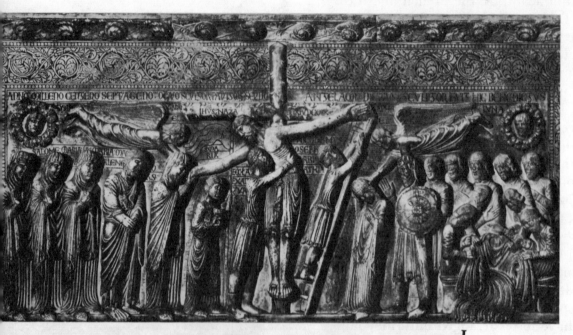

1

2

The Italian sculpture showing the Deposition from the Cross, 1, and the Indian sculpture, 2, of Buddha's first sermon to his comrades seem at a first glance to have nothing in common. They are, however, very much alike in feeling and vary in detail only. The plant forms are different because they come from different countries; the human bodies are in different postures, and this too we must expect. But the central positions of the figures of Christ and Buddha, the interest in the rhythm of the figures around them contained in borders of plant forms, in short the feeling for pattern is the same in both. See how similar are the patterns of folds in the garments.

3 **4**

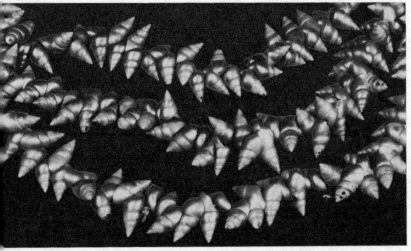

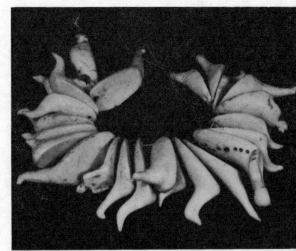

As we have already seen, when natural objects are brought into a pattern their shapes are often changed. This change may be so great that the original shapes are difficult or even impossible to recognise. Look at the two necklaces, **3, 4**. The first one, of shells, shows natural objects arranged in a pattern but not changed in any way. Picture **4**, shows a necklace of ivory pieces, each carved in the shape of a bird. These bird shapes have been changed a little and made simpler. This is the first step in a process called *abstraction*. The wood carvings, **5**, show how a natural shape—a lizard—may be gradually changed until it becomes abstract. The stone carvings, **6, 7**, also show

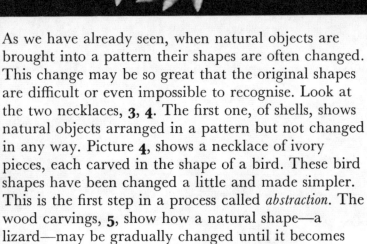

5

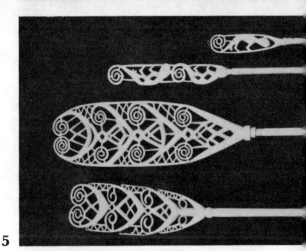

6

7

abstractions—of different plant shapes. Abstraction has been used by man from earliest times. This Greek pattern, **8**, may seem just a pleasant piece of decoration to you but to the artist it was more than that, it represented the sea and the rolling waves. The artist who first used this pattern left out everything that was not absolutely necessary for his purpose. The pattern does not show us the actual waves but in spite of that we can feel the forward movement of each breaker.

8

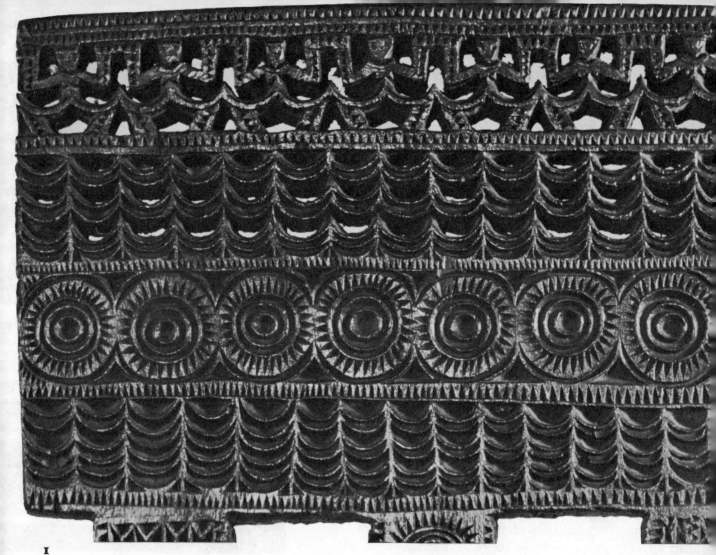

I

This Polynesian carving, **1**, gives us another example
of how abstraction may come about. The top strip
shows a row of human figures. In the second strip,
wishing to stress their pattern and movement the artist
has left out everything unnecessary to his purpose.
The result is an abstract pattern which we might not
have recognised if we had not seen the top strip.
There are, of course, many different kinds of
abstraction and many different reasons for them. For
example, before money was invented, people bartered
(exchanged) goods instead of buying and selling.
All kinds of things were used in barter: animals, skins,
tools. Spear-heads were often especially prized and in
demand. Sometimes a man might exchange an
animal for a certain number of spear-heads. He would
then exchange the spear-heads for a set of tools which

he needed. In these exchanges he was using the spear-heads not for their original purpose but in the same way as we use money. A cow might be worth four spear-heads and a calf only two. When the idea of money finally evolved it was first made in the shape of spear-heads, **2**. These pieces of metal could not be used as real spear-heads for hunting: they merely *represent* the value of real spear-heads. As you can see in the picture, the token spear-heads have the advantage of fitting neatly together when there are several of them.

You will find many examples of abstraction in your daily life. Your mathematics books are full of them. You can see one on every road sign. What do you think is the reason for using abstractions rather than detailed drawings or even photographs?

When people first started to express sounds in writing they used shapes suggested by their surroundings. The diagram, **3**, shows how some of these shapes were gradually changed until they became letters of our alphabet. We can say, then, that our letters are abstractions of natural forms.

Below you see two maps of the London Underground. The one on the left is an accurate map, the one on the right may be said to be an abstraction. If you wanted to find your way quickly, which would you choose?

2

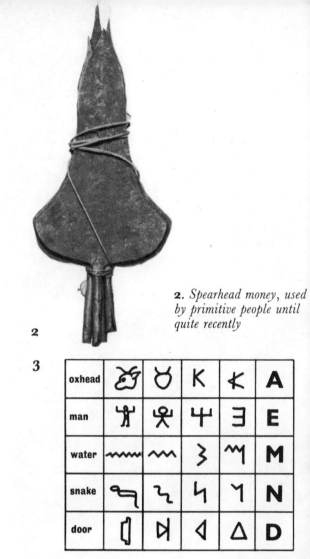

2. Spearhead money, used by primitive people until quite recently

3

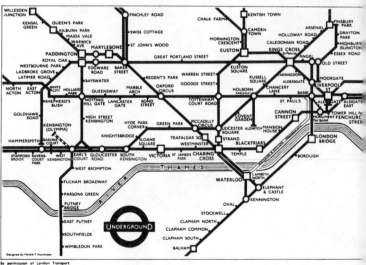

oxhead				A
man				E
water				M
snake				N
door				D

4   5

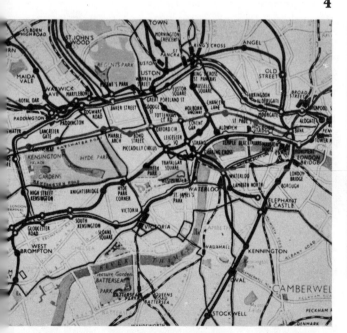

1. Section through a bone, magnified 40 times
3. Zinc oxide seen under the microscope

1   2

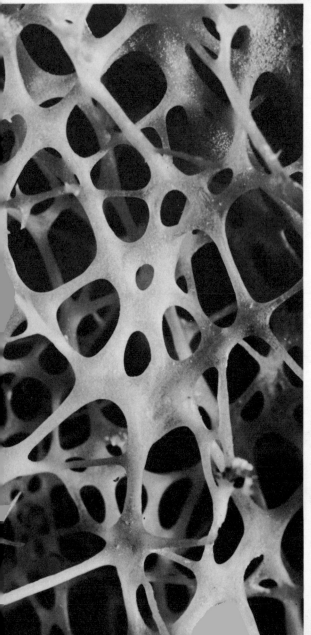

In modern times and thanks to recent inventions we have seen things which have never before been seen by man. Our microscopes, telescopes, cameras and other powerful machines help us to see things invisible to the naked eye. Through these machines we are discovering more and more about the natural world. We are becoming more and more familiar with shapes and patterns which would have been meaningless fifty years ago. Today these new shapes are part of our lives. We see them in books, magazines, on television, even on posters. As we become more and more familiar with them, we are bringing them into our patterns. You can see from pictures **4** to **8** that atomic patterns can look just as interesting as flower patterns. We have never seen structures like these before, yet we recognise them as natural shapes. There is then no real difference between these new patterns and all the others we have so far discussed. They are all taken from man's surroundings. Any aspect of nature can provide an idea for a pattern.

3

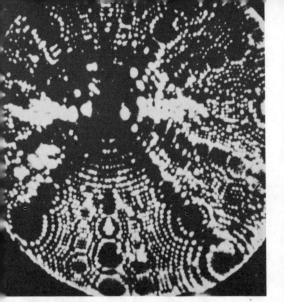

4 5

*A photograph of a cluster of atoms, 4,
magnified 2,750,000 times, and the
printed pattern, 5, which was derived
from it. The patterns of these two pieces
of lace, 6, were derived from diagrams,
7 and 8, of crystal structures (that is,
the way in which crystals are arranged)
of haemoglobin (circular) and polythene
(wavy).*

6

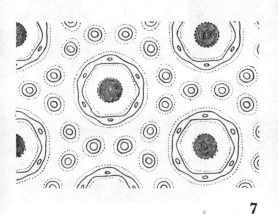

7

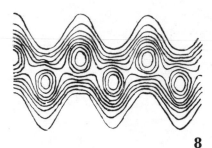

8

Patterns which develop from natural and familiar objects in man's surroundings vary from country to country. Abstract patterns originate in familiar objects. Today powerful instruments are revealing hitherto unseen natural shapes, which as they grow more familiar are also used in patterns.

EXERCISES

1. Would you think it right if the Eskimos tried to make patterns of vine leaves or the Greeks patterns of reindeer?

2. Do you think picture **1** shows a modern pattern? Why?

3. Pictures **2** and **3** both show Samoan patterns. Which do you think is the more abstract?

1. *A modern wallpaper*
2 *and* **3.** *Samoan patterns made with b*

1

4. What do we mean when we say that pictures **2** to **8** on pages 32 and 33 show *natural* shapes?

5. Choose some natural shapes and make them into an abstract pattern.

6. The abstract pattern in the second strip of picture **1** on page 30 expresses the movement of the human figures better than the more realistic top strip. Explain the reasons for the three examples of abstraction on page 31. Try to find other abstractions and to explain them.

2 3

4

Town and country patterns

So far most of the man-made patterns we have looked at have been intended as decoration. We have, however, already met a few man-made patterns not planned as decorations. These are often part of an object's construction, the pattern of brickwork for example. One sees this kind of pattern more often than the intentionally decorative kind. Many such patterns are formed when similar things are grouped together; the pattern of milk bottles, **1**, or the pattern of loaves and rolls, **2**, strung up to form a screen. In picture **3** the bricks are stacked up, waiting to be used. In picture **4** they have been built into a wall. Why do you think all brick walls show this kind of pattern? If you interlock your fingers so that they overlap each other, you will find that your hands are quite firmly linked. The wall holds together because the bricks overlap horizontally. It is, of course, possible to build a wall arranging bricks in many different ways and without overlapping. One could build in the pattern of the stacked bricks, **3**, for instance, but such a wall would not be strong. There is only one satisfactory way of using bricks to make a strong wall and that is to interlock them. Picture **4** shows a typical pattern of interlocked bricks.

2

3 4

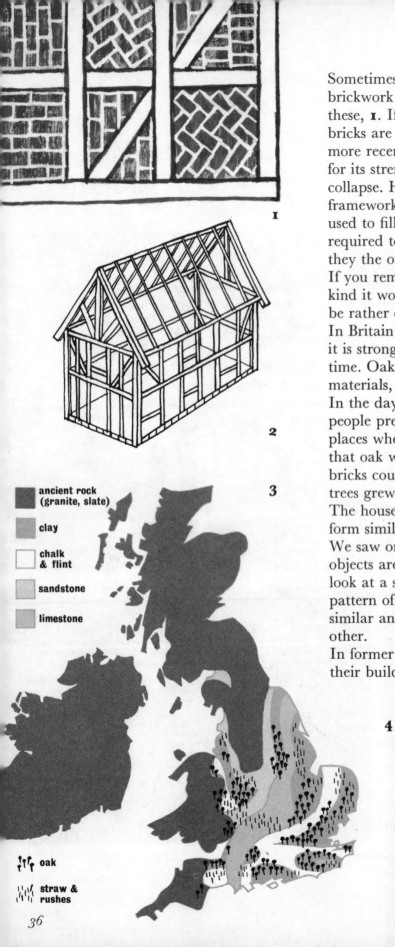

1

2

3

- ■ ancient rock (granite, slate)
- ■ clay
- □ chalk & flint
- ■ sandstone
- ■ limestone

oak

straw & rushes

Sometimes, on very old buildings, you can see brickwork in which the patterns are arranged like these, **1**. If you look carefully, you will see that these bricks are not used to make the kind of wall we see in more recent buildings. A modern house which relied for its strength on walls like these would certainly collapse. Houses were at one time built with a wooden framework, **2**, to hold them together, and bricks were used to fill in the spaces. The bricks were not required to bear the weight of the house, nor were they the only material used for filling in the framework. If you removed all the bricks from a house of this kind it would still remain standing although it would be rather draughty.

In Britain the best timber for building is oak because it is strong, stands up to the weather, and lasts a long time. Oak trees grow best on clay soil, so that the two materials, oak and clay, are usually found together. In the days before there was a good transport system, people preferred to use materials available near the places where they planned to build. It was discovered that oak was the best timber for building and that bricks could be made from the clay on which the oak trees grew. Men accordingly used the two together, **4**. The houses they constructed of these two materials form similar patterns wherever they are found.

We saw on page 35 that when a number of similar objects are grouped together a pattern is formed. To look at a street like the one in picture **5** is to look at a pattern of this kind. The construction of the houses is similar and their shapes differ only slightly from each other.

In former times, when men used local materials for their building much more than is done today, the

4

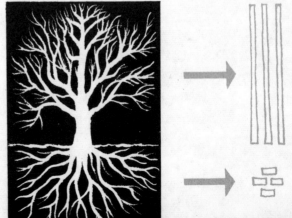

appearance of towns and villages was an expression of the countryside. In those parts of the country where there was no clay, and bricks were therefore scarce, other building materials were used. Chalk by itself is not very suitable for building, but the flints which are found in chalk make good walls, and the chalk can be used to make plaster which is excellent for covering the flint walls. Chalk used in this way produced a method of decorating houses called pargetting. You can see examples of this decoration, found only in chalk districts, in pictures **6** and **7**.

5
6

7

I **2**

Limestone is one of the best building stones and can be hewn into many different shapes. Although it is soft enough for easy working, yet it is hard enough to withstand the weather over many centuries. This mullion window, **I**, would not have been made of a hard stone like granite. Such windows help to give a limestone village, **2**, its characteristic pattern. Granite by contrast is difficult to work, and houses in granite districts are very simple. Compare the granite cottages, **3**, with picture **2**.

3

2. *Limestone houses in Chipping Campden.* **3.** *Granite cottages near Lands End*

4

These houses from different parts of the world show how man's choice of building material is governed by his surroundings. Some of the constructions may look strange to you, but their patterns are the result of the most efficient use of the materials for a particular purpose: Mexican houses, **4**, made of branches, clay and straw, with flat roofs and few windows, for life in a hot, dry land; Zulu huts, **5**, made of a curved basket-like framework of reeds, which is covered with grass; houses in Sumatra, **6**, made of canes and wood, with their steep roofs, designed to deal with sudden torrential downpours.

5

6

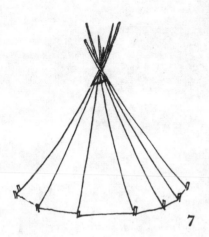

7

7. *Red Indian tent made of skins and sticks.* **8.** *Liberian hut made of mud, sticks and foliage*

When man cultivates the ground, his material is the land with its covering of soil. Just as building materials vary throughout the world, so does the land. Soil may be light or heavy, dry or waterlogged. In some parts the land lies flat in plains, in others it is piled up in steep mountains. A farmer's material is the land and whatever it may be like he must make the best use of it. Pictures **1** and **2** show different ways in which people manage to get the best from the land. The level Dutch land, with few natural obstacles, can easily be divided by straight lines, **1**. The Dutch farmer needs to drain his fields, to prevent flooding, and he must build dykes to protect them from the sea. The Formosa countryside is quite different, **2**. The Formosan farmer cannot divide his mountainous land with straight boundaries. Because of the steep mountain

1

slopes the water would run away if it were not prevented, carrying the soil with it. The farmer has to build low walls to retain the soil and the water. Each wall must keep to the same level. That is why the walls wind their way round the hills and mountains like the contour lines on a map. Both the Dutch farmer and the Formosan farmer have the same object: to grow food. They have both learnt to get the most out of their land, but because of the difference in their material they have drawn different patterns on the countryside. Compare this with two builders, one making a wall with flints, the other with bricks. Both build well, but because of the difference in their materials the patterns of the two walls are different.

You can see in picture **1** that all the fields in the Dutch landscape look very much alike. The farms too are similar, **3**. This is only to be expected, for over the

3

centuries farmers have learnt the best way of cultivating this kind of land and have imposed a characteristic pattern on the countryside. When the same material is used for the same purpose, the patterns made are similar. That is why the Formosan fields and farms also resemble each other and are part of a characteristic pattern.

We have seen that the pattern of tilled fields depends on the land, just as the pattern of a wall depends on the material used in its construction. But man's building materials also depend on the land, for it is the source of those materials: stone, timber, clay, and so on. So the fields man tills and the houses he builds have their material in common. We have already found that, with something in common, things go together pleasantly: the timber-framed houses, the native huts, or the Formosan fields.

A landscape seems beautiful when the things in it have something in common: this gives a unity to the whole. Look at these pictures. First the fragment of Italian landscape, 1. The beautiful pattern of the tilled fields clinging to the hilly slopes runs right through this countryside, holding everything together. The houses, made of materials found in the hills, fit into that pattern. Then there is the pattern of the vegetation: olive groves, vineyards and groups of cypresses. Because they are all born of the same earth, these patterns fit together and form one larger pattern of great beauty.

Now compare this Italian scene to the English landscape, 3. These gentle hills with their fields also make a pattern, quite different from the Italian one but no less beautiful. This pattern, too, runs right through the landscape and knits it together. The houses, built of stone quarried in the hills, fit into their background, and the trees add yet another interesting pattern to the whole. Both the Italian and the English landscapes are lovely, each in its way. But natural patterns are often upset by man. Can you say how the natural patterns have been disturbed in picture 4? Do you think it matters when man changes the natural patterns of his surroundings? You will remember the relationship that exists between our surroundings and the patterns we make; how they cause us to make

2. *Sheds like this one made of Tuscan cane are part of the pattern of the Tuscan landscape.*

3

4

patterns of a certain kind. But the importance of our surroundings does not end there. They affect us more deeply than we realise. Mountain people are different from people who live in the plains. Country people are different from town people. When the patterns of his surroundings are changed man too is certain to change. This change may take a long time but it is inevitable. That is why we must be careful in altering our surroundings if our natures are not to be changed for the worse.

When you see an industrial landscape, **4**, do you ever wonder how the pleasant pattern shown in picture **1** was changed into a pattern so unpleasant? It all took place gradually. This series of pictures, **2**, shows what probably happened.

During the years that Oldham, **1** and **4**, and many other industrial towns were expanding, few people cared about the disfigurement of the countryside. Today we understand much better that, in planning and building our industrial towns, we must take care not to harm our surroundings.

1

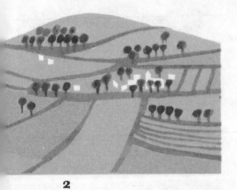  

2

3

44

Oldham, Lancashire, as it was in 1780, **1**, and as it is today, **4**. As a result of the Industrial Revolution, factories went up everywhere, **3**, dominating the countryside and the new towns, while living quarters were largely thought of as a necessary evil, **5**, and as little space as possible was squandered on them.

5

1

Why do nineteenth-century industrial towns disfigure the countryside, whereas ancient towns and villages add to its beauty? Before the Industrial Revolution villages and market towns, growing gradually through the centuries, were built by people who understood the countryside. That is why they fit into its pattern so well. Towards the end of the eighteenth century, when large scale manufacturing was introduced, certain existing towns were hastily expanded to accommodate it. Buildings were put up rapidly, when and where they were wanted, without any idea of planning for future needs. This lack of planning resulted in inefficiency and ugliness. Such towns remain as blots on the landscape because they were imposed upon the countryside by people who had lost all touch with it. By contrast, designers of good modern industrial towns work with and not against the countryside; they do not ignore it like their

1. *Palmanova, an Italian town, organised and fortified by military engineers. Although the town's pattern is good in itself, it is a misfit, out of keeping with the surrounding countryside. But towns and villages which have been allowed to grow up naturally fit into the pattern of the countryside,* 2.

2

nineteenth-century forerunners. Pictures **3**, **4** and **5** show modern industrial towns which have been designed especially for their purpose. Everything is well placed and combines happily. The towns are efficient and each makes a satisfactory pattern. Wherever we look in towns like these we see a pleasant vista. Can you see how Peterlee fits into the landscape, **4**? An industrial town need not disfigure its surroundings; it can even add something of value to them.

3. *The Market Square of Harlow New Town.* **4, 5.** *Houses in Peterlee, Durham. Compare them with houses on page 45.*

5

4

I

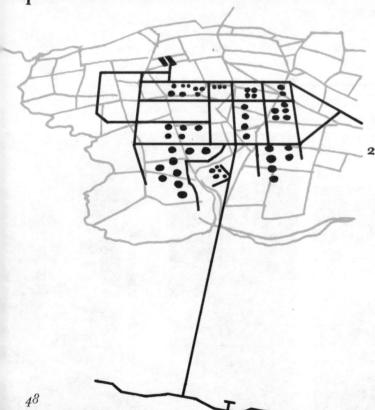

Industrial installations can be made to fit into the pattern of the landscape. The B.P. installation at Milford Haven in South Wales, **1**, and the French hydro-electric dam, **3**, fit naturally into the existing pattern. The drawing, **2**, however, shows a series of installations wilfully imposed on the countryside.

2

3

TO SUM UP

We can sometimes tell whether materials have been put to good or bad use by the patterns which are formed. Objects made of the same material have patterns in common, and because of this underlying unity a group of objects made of the same material forms a larger pattern of its own. Different materials make different patterns.

EXERCISES

1. You saw how the pattern of the stacked bricks changed when they were used in a wall. Can you find any other patterns which change in a similar way?
2. These cottages, **4,** are rather like the Cornish cottages which you saw on page 38. Can you explain why?
3. Here is the English landscape, **5,** but this picture shows the pattern only. Draw a pattern like this of the place where you live.
4. Can you learn from the map on page 36 in which parts of England you are likely to see thatched roofs?
5. The division of the country by different methods of building is not nearly as definite as it used to be. What caused this change? What have the railways to do with it?

4

5

5

The same and yet different

Have you ever looked at a modern building like the one in picture **1** before? How does it strike you? Would you like to live in a street of buildings like this? The windows are all the same size. The spaces between them are all the same. There are hundreds of windows going on and on, seemingly for ever. What do you think of it? How does it make you feel? What about the buildings in the pictures **2** and **3**? What do you feel about them? It does not really matter where they are and when they were built; look at them as good or bad patterns, just as you looked at the countryside and houses in the last chapter. The building in picture **2** is quite different from the modern building, **1**. It has no repetition. The windows are all different, the spaces between the windows are different, the roof is made up of many different parts, and even the façade is broken up into many sections which come forward or go back, and add to the irregularity of the building. Do you like this building better than **1**? Do you think it is too much of a muddle? What do you think of **3**? This building has no unending repeats, nor is it made up of parts which are all different. Do you think it is more pleasant to look at than the other two? Which of these buildings would you choose to live in?

Before we judge these buildings we must find out something more about pattern. We have been looking at many patterns and deciding why there are good or bad. Now let us try and think what patterns mean to us.

Imagine you have emptied a box of matches on to a table. You will be faced with a pattern like **4**.

Most people when they see a mess like this want to put it into some sort of order. If you had nothing better to do you would probably start to arrange the matches in a pattern, perhaps like the one in **5**. If somebody came along and told you that your pattern was not nearly even enough, what would you do? You might try to improve it, straighten each match stick, and line them up in rows from left to right and then from top to bottom. But in the end your pattern would still not be absolutely regular. Look closely at the ordinary piece of expanded metal shown in picture **6**. You can see that there is not a single unevenness in the pattern. But picture **6** shows only a small piece of metal. The machine which made it must have produced thousands of yards of the same pattern without a single flaw. No one could have done

3

4

6

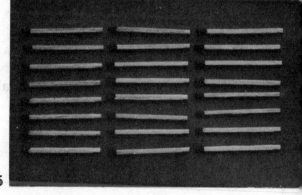

5

this by hand. Man cannot repeat anything with absolute regularity, as the matchstick pattern, **5**, showed. He cannot even sign his name in exactly the same way twice. Yet a machine built by man can repeat the most complicated patterns with perfect accuracy. Let us think about this.

When we look at a crowd of people from a distance they all look alike. If you look across a football ground at the spectators on the other side all you can see is a pattern of white round shapes which seem to be the same shape repeated again and again. But if you look at the people near you, you will get quite a different impression. These people look quite different from each other. Some have round faces, some long, some have pointed chins, some have high foreheads, some people's hair is straight, others curly. No two people are identical, and yet we are all alike: we all have two eyes, one nose, one mouth and so on. The shapes of eyes, nose and mouth are basically the same, but they vary slightly from person to person. All human bodies show the same basic similarity: we are all constructed in the same way but in spite of this we all look different; some people are short, some tall, some thin, some fat, and so on.

This basic similarity of construction combined with differences of detail is characteristic of all living things.

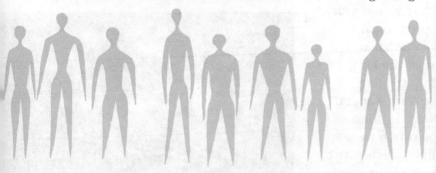

Take a number of leaves from the same tree and you will find no two are exactly the same shape, although they all look alike. The construction of each leaf is the same, the veins are arranged in the same way, but the shapes are not repeated exactly. Peas in a pod are supposed to be exactly alike but they too all have different shapes. And if you look really hard you will

find that even eggs vary in shape. This is the way nature builds. It is as though she had an idea of how to make a thing but could not repeat it exactly every

time. You will remember that when you made your matchstick pattern you too had an idea of how to build your pattern, but you could not be as exact about it as you would have liked to be. Man is part of nature, just as leaves, peas and eggs are. That is why, like nature herself, he cannot make two identical things. In thinking about the similarity of objects, there are two different things to be borne in mind: construction and shape. A construction is often repeated in nature, but a shape never. If we see a thousand apples on a tree, we can be sure that they are all different. Each apple will delight our eyes in a different way. Nature is never dull, no matter how many times she repeats her constructions. If you look at human hands you will see that they are all different. The construction is, of course, the same for every hand: four fingers and a thumb, three joints to each finger and two to each thumb. But the shapes of all the hands are different.

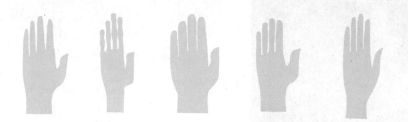

You read on page 51 that a man never writes his name in exactly the same way twice. In spite of this, you can recognise his signature whenever you see it. His handwriting has its own character and is different from the handwriting of every other human being. Let us see why.

a

a a a a a a a

When you first learnt to write your teacher probably wrote a number of letters on the blackboard for the class to copy. Let us say she wrote a letter 'a'. You all tried to copy his letter faithfully, but did every member of the class produce exactly the same result? Of course not, because you all had different hands, and different muscles and different minds to guide your hands. Some of you made wide letters, some narrow ones, some squarish ones. You all made different shapes, but in spite of this anybody could have recognised them because the basic construction was always the same. These differences were not caused only by your lack of experience in writing. People who have been writing for many years still write differently from each other. In the same way, no two people ever make identical objects.

We know that nothing is ever repeated exactly in the world of nature, and men, who are part of nature, are all different. It is therefore not surprising that variety pleases us and that we do not like absolute regularity. But we do not like muddle either. Nature is orderly (remember how often she repeats the same construction), but her shapes and patterns have an infinite variety. We like order, but we need variation within that order. We should think there was something wrong if all the leaves on a tree were exactly alike or if all the petals of a flower were identical. But we should think something was equally wrong if we could not recognise the family likenesses of the leaves or the petals.

Now you will understand why pattern **5** on page 13 is so much more pleasant than pattern **6**. Pattern **5** is made up of shapes which are all slightly different but which have the same construction. The shapes of the other pattern are all different and give us a feeling of muddle.

Let us now look again at the three buildings illustrated on pages 50 and 51. Which of the three has order without deadening repetition? Only that one will be in tune with nature and therefore also in tune with us. Building **1** has too much in common with the piece of expanded metal. We said that we should feel something had gone wrong if all the petals of a flower were exactly the same; it would not please us. Why

1

2

54

This is a detail of the building on page 51. You can see that although there is a constant change of patterns and even of surfaces everything belongs together.

3

then should hundreds of windows like this please us? It is out of keeping with nature and therefore also out of keeping with us. Building **2** is a muddle, following no orderly plan of construction, and since there is no muddle in nature this building too is out of keeping with nature.

Now that we have found out a little more about what patterns mean to us, what do you think of building **3**? This building has no tiring repetition, but it has no muddle either. The windows are all similar, but not exactly the same. They look as though they belong to the same family. In this they are like the leaves on the tree. They are arranged in a pleasing, uneven pattern. The expanse of wall is broken up into smaller areas without destroying the unity of the whole design. Compare this pleasant irregularity with the muddle in building **2**. Building **3** is without a doubt the best. We have discovered why building **1** is unsatisfactory, but we have seen that modern ways of building can sometimes lend themselves to making shapes which are in tune with nature, **3**. When man ignores the laws of nature, the result is ugliness. If we are to make beautiful buildings (or indeed anything beautiful) they must be in keeping with nature. The modern buildings in pictures **3**, **4** and **5** show that this can be done. Each of these buildings gives us a strong feeling of unity of construction, while the details of each building offer pleasantly varied patterns which yet belong together, as the apples on one tree belong together.

4

5

TO SUM UP

We are part of nature. Nature repeats constructions but she never repeats a shape exactly. We too obey this law: we cannot make things which are exactly alike. When we make things we should try to follow nature's plan.

EXERCISES

1. Make drawings of three leaves of the same tree, three flowers of the same plant and three apples of the same kind. How are they similar and how do they vary? Notice specially the construction of the leaves, flowers and apples.

2. You have seen how in the past the unity of patterns of villages and towns was largely brought about through the use of the same building materials. Streets then never looked like picture **1**. Why not? Why do they now?

3. The houses in this street, **2**, have been built in the last few years. Do you like the street, or do you think there is something wrong with it?

4. Why do people build houses like those in picture **2**?

5. Picture **3** is a drawing by an American cartoonist. What point does it make?

1

2

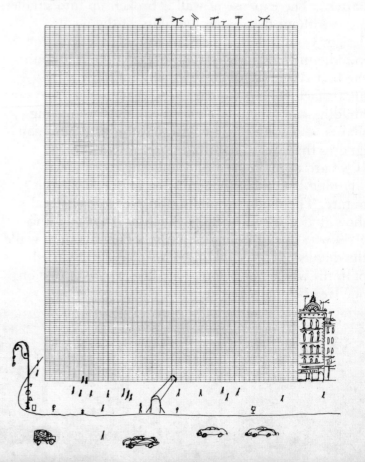

3

56

6

A half way chapter

Machines, when used intelligently, can produce not only useful but beautiful things which could not have been produced by any other means. Used without understanding and imagination they create ugly and inhuman surroundings for all of us. Patterns **1, 2** and **3** have a strange, almost magical beauty. They were produced by complicated electronic machines and they are as typical of our machine age as pattern **6** on page 51.

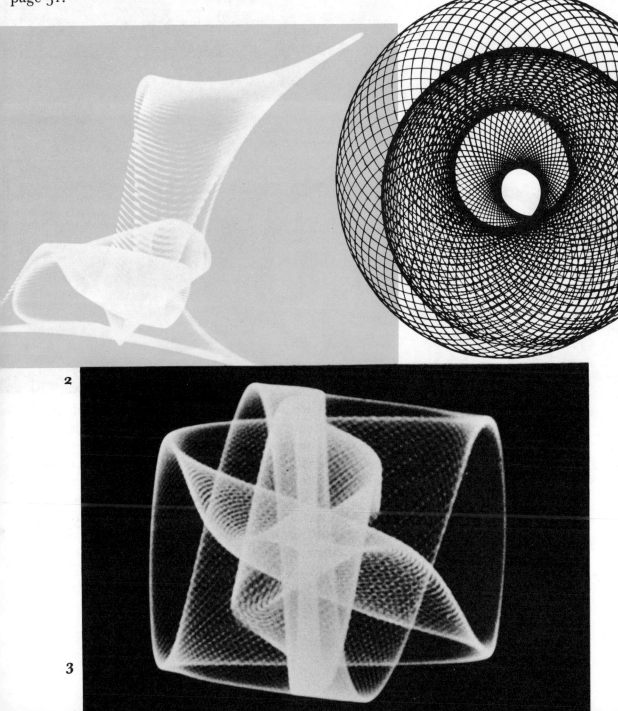

1

2

3

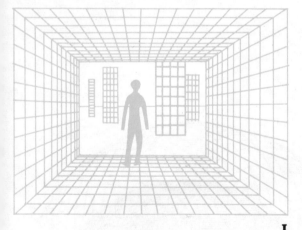

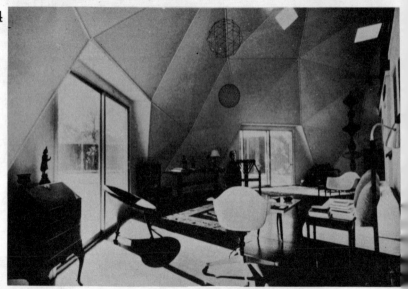

1 2

3 4

2. Building with prefabricated parts in China
3. Transporting the framework of a prefabricated house by helicopter in the U.S.A. and, **4,** *a room in such a house*

At a time when so many of our goods are machine-made we must expect repetitive patterns, for this is the way of the machine. Even houses are now built of mass-produced parts and this process of mechanisation is likely to continue and increase. If we allow our machines to churn out the wrong sort of patterns, at odds with our inborn feeling for natural patterns, unsuited to their materials, out of keeping with our surroundings, we shall in a short time create the kind of environment in which no human being can live happily, **1**. What can we do to make our machines produce the patterns which we need?

This Gothic roof, **5**, was designed for stone. If we learn to design for the materials of our age, for reinforced concrete, for steel, for glass, for plastics, we shall construct patterns which are beautiful because they are suited to their materials. Patterns **6**, **7** and **8** are quite different from each other—because they are made of different materials, properly used—and each is beautiful in its own way.

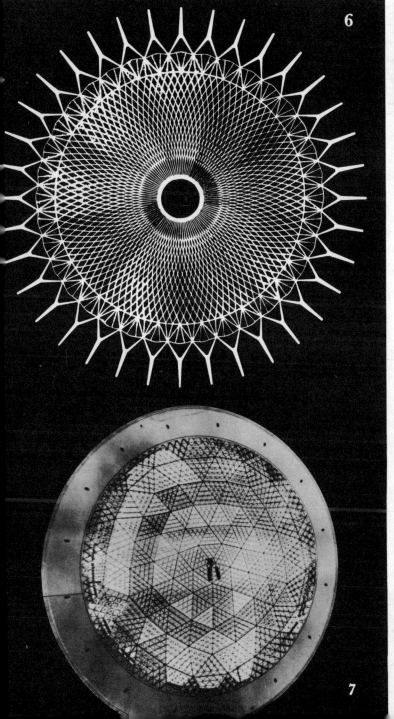

5. *The roof of a Gothic church.* **6**. *The reinforced concrete roof of the smaller Sports Palace in Rome shown on page 23, and,* **7**, *a roof made of glass and steel.*

8. *The pattern of the metal case of this modern Italian demijohn is different from the pattern of the old-fashioned cases, which were usually made of rush or wickerwork.*

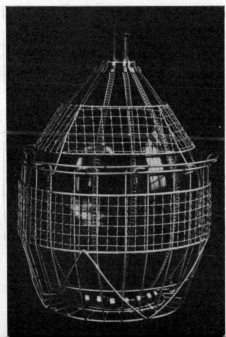

Care in mixing patterns is very important. For instance, by planting trees of the same size and kind at regular intervals, **1**, the monotonous, grid-like pattern of a modern building is stressed. Trees planted with imagination, **2**, can break the monotony of such a background and blend happily with it; the two patterns support each other. The geometric pattern of the building sets off the plant forms to full advantage and the pattern of the trees makes the building look better. In the same way a geometric wallpaper, **3**, combines well with plant forms, **4**, while a wallpaper derived from natural patterns, **5**, will blend well with angular shapes.

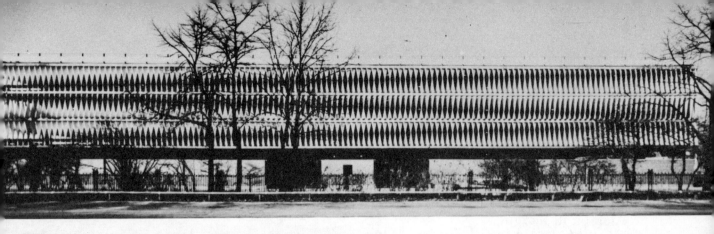

The twisted sheets of reinforced concrete on this parking garage, **6**, **7**, act as shades from the sun. At the same time they make a most unusual pattern. Machine-made parts are here used in such a way that usefulness and pleasantness are combined. With imagination and ingenuity man can use machines to produce objects with patterns of the kind he needs. Machine-made patterns have invaded most parts of our lives and in many different ways. We have seen that many of our industrial towns have upset the natural pattern of the countryside, but there are other offenders. Roads for fast-moving traffic can spoil whole stretches of country, but they need not do so. The road in picture **8** is certainly efficient, yet it does not spoil the countryside. Some people might even say that it makes it more interesting to look at.

People make different patterns because their surroundings are different. In making their patterns they use familiar objects, just as a poet uses his mother tongue and not a foreign language. Here is the beginning of a poem:

> I saw three witches
> That bowed down like barley,
> And took to their brooms 'neath a louring sky,
> And, mounting a storm-cloud,
> Aloft on its margin,
> Stood black in the silver as up they did fly.
>
> I saw three witches
> That mocked the poor sparrows
> They carried in cages of wicker along,
> Till a hawk from his eyrie
> Swooped down like an arrow,
> And smote on the cages, and ended their song.

These lines may not look like a pattern to you, but if you read them aloud you will *hear* the pattern. A poem is a pattern in sound. You cannot see the rhythmic pattern, you can only hear it. Before you can write a good poem you must know a language very well and even be able to take liberties with it. Can you find a word that this poet has changed (distorted) to fit the pattern? Generally speaking nobody can make a satisfactory pattern of any kind if he is not familiar with the things he uses to make it.

We cannot always understand at first sight the patterns made by people of other countries. Such patterns seem strange to us until we know something about the surroundings which produced them. The

Music consists of patterns of sounds. 1 shows part of an orchestral score. Even if you cannot read music you will get a fair idea of the pattern the composer had in mind. 2 is a piece of keyboard music. Although there are fewer notes to be played at the same time than in the orchestral music, the pattern is much more complicated. A short tune, called the subject (in colour), is repeated in various ways which fit together, like the many other patterns we have looked at. Sometimes the subject is repeated, turned upside down or with other changes, and such musical patterns can be extremely ingenious and complicated.

I   2

Flutes
Clarinets
Bassoons
Horns
Trumpets
Drums
First violins
Second violins
Violas
Cellos and double basses

3 4

effect of our surroundings goes much deeper than most of us realise. The Gothic style of building, **3** and **4**, was born in Northern Europe, where the pattern of the Northern forests influenced its creators, and it is difficult to imagine it belonging to any other part of the world. Gothic architects did not consciously imitate the forests, but the pattern of the trees which surrounded those early builders so impressed itself on their minds that it reappeared in the style of their buildings.

Perhaps there is a similar connection between Indian architecture, **6**, and the layer-like nature of many Indian rock formations, **7**.

5

6   7

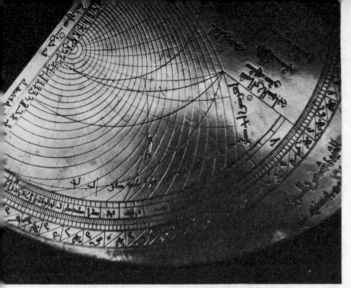

Our activities and the kind of lives we lead can also
influence the patterns we make. The two Islamic
patterns of about the tenth century, **1** and **2,** are both
engraved on brass, but picture **1** shows an instrument
used in astronomy, while the object in picture **2** is
part of a dish and shows a typical decorative pattern
of the same period. The pattern on the dish is not
an imitation of the instrument, but it is quite likely
that the Arabs' interest in astronomy and their use of
scientific diagrams influenced the kind of patterns
they made.

Some of our own patterns show clearly the influence

3

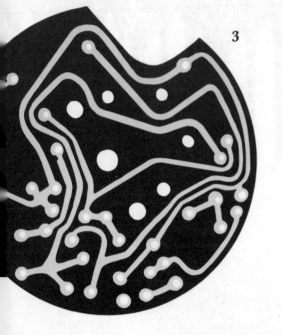

4

of our daily activities. The pattern of this wallpaper,
4, was probably not a conscious imitation of the
pattern of the printed circuit used in radio sets, **3,** but
it appeals to people familiar with such patterns. What

5

does the wallpaper in picture **5** remind you of? One cannot imagine such patterns being made a hundred or two hundred years ago.

Patterns, as you have now discovered, are also affected by their materials; the development of writing offers good examples of this. Egyptian hieroglyphics, **6**, consisted of pictures taken from life. These shapes, designed for carving, were found too cumbersome when the Egyptians started to write in ink on papyrus, and so they gradually changed, **8**. The Assyrians wrote on clay, which they made into writing tablets, **7**. At first the letters were scratched into the soft clay but this method did not prove satisfactory. Eventually a style of writing called cuneiform was evolved in which each letter consisted of a number of separate impressions made with the end of a writing tool, **9**. The chart, **10**, shows how Assyrian letterforms changed as the scribes became more skilled in the use of their material and tools.

8

9

7

10

fish				
ox				
grain				
sun				

This chart, **1**, illustrates the development of Chinese writing which, like the Egyptian and Assyrian, shows the influence of writing materials, in this case brush, ink and paper, on the design of the letter forms. In the same way, italic writing owes the shape of its letters to the use of the quill pen, **2**. Letter forms, originating as pictures taken from man's surroundings, were shaped over the centuries by the use of different materials and different tools.

no matter if it shattered th
bird with harsh discord
bulged with brightness;
the twig or rail. They sa
shelter, to the air and the

1   **2**

3   **4**

3. *A pen drawing, and* **4**, *a brush drawing, both by Rembrandt*

EXERCISES

1. Using materials well is called *efficiency*. The bricks in the brick wall are used efficiently; they could not be arranged better. Any change in the pattern would weaken the wall. Here are two efficient patterns, **5**, **6**. Can you find other examples of efficient patterns?

2. In this row of huts, **7**, all but one of the shapes are similar because with this one exception the building materials have been used efficiently. One of the villagers tried to use the materials in a different way and built his house in the shape of a square hut. Why do you think these huts are normally built in the round shape? Do you think the square one would be as strong as the others?

3. Suppose a Dutch farmer went on a holiday to Formosa and liked the interesting shapes of the fields so much that when he returned to Holland he re-shaped all his fields in the Formosan pattern, **8**. What do you think would happen? And suppose that a Formosan farmer was so taken by the clean and simple pattern of the Dutch landscape that he remodelled all his fields and made them rectangular, **9**. What would happen then? Would each gain or lose? What can you learn from this?

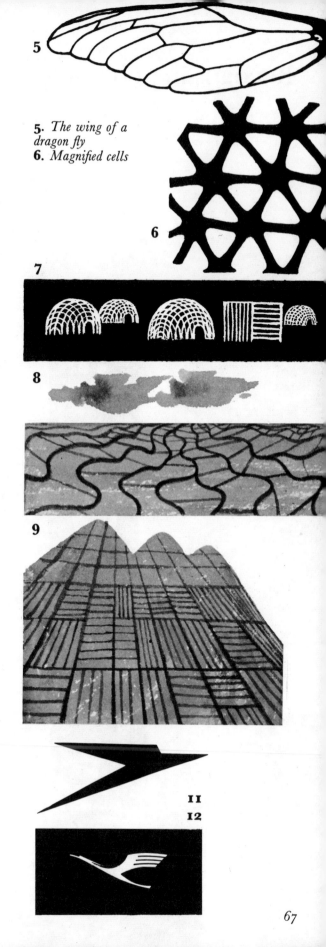

5. *The wing of a dragon fly*
6. *Magnified cells*

10

4. Why are marble churches like the one in picture **10** fairly common in Italy but rarely seen in other countries?

5. Why do you think air lines use abstractions like **11** and **12** for their trademarks? Which do you prefer?

6. You have seen how patterns change when the materials of which they are made change. Find some patterns which have changed in this way.

7. Can you think of ways in which man disfigures the countryside?

Recognising character

Imagine that you are away on holiday with a certain sum of money to spend. Suppose that you spend eightpence of this money on the first day, ninepence on the following day, while on the third day you spend only fourpence. What would your reply be if someone asked you how much you had been spending per day? To answer this question you would need to work out the average amount you had spent on any one day. The way to do this is to add up all the money you have spent over the three days and then to divide the total by the number of days. Altogether you have spent one shilling and ninepence. When you divide this by three, you get the answer sevenpence, so that sevenpence is the average amount you have spent per day.

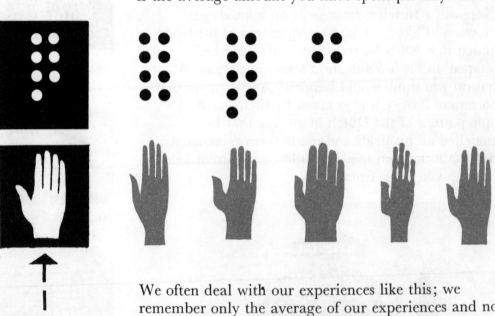

We often deal with our experiences like this; we remember only the average of our experiences and not each single one. If, for instance, you hear the word 'hand' you will think of a shape like the one on the black background. This is not an actual hand but an average of all the hands you have ever seen: what we might call the idea of a hand. If you look at real hands you will see that although their construction is always the same, every hand has something which distinguishes it from your idea of a hand. This something is called *character*. All the coloured hands in this row have character because they are all different from the average. The more an object varies from the average the more character it has.

hand →

When a baker makes bread rolls he has a certain shape in mind and tries to make them all to that shape. But they come out of the oven in different shapes. Most of the rolls will be more or less the same but there will be an occasional one which is less like the shape the baker thought of than the others. It is only the odd rolls, the ones with most character, which you would recognise if you saw them again. Character helps us to recognise things. You have probably heard the word character applied to human beings. What does it mean when someone is described as 'quite a character'?

You know that human beings not only look different but also have different ways of doing things. They write differently, speak differently, have different

ways of walking, eating, sleeping, or joking. One of your acquaintances may be lazier than anyone else you know; laziness is part of his character. Somebody else may be the most honest person you know; honesty is an important part of his character. Character influences everything a person does. Handwriting is an example of this. We are all taught the same shapes when we first learn to write, but we all write them differently, according to our individual character. Telling a story is another example of the influence of character. If several people hear the same story each one of them retells it in a slightly different way. Each one gives the story a little bit of his character.

These children are watching the same event but each one shows different feelings.

Picture **1** shows the shape of the average house but of course no real house looks like this, any more than a real hand is like your idea of a hand. The houses in Amsterdam, **2**, Chipping Campden, **3**, and Venice, **4**, have the same construction as the average house, but they vary a great deal in detail. It is these variations which give the three towns their characteristic patterns. In picture **5**, of Hanley, the characteristic pattern is produced by the interspersing of kilns with the houses. Try to recall a town you have visited. You will probably find that what comes first to your mind is its characteristic pattern.

1

3

5

Here are two photographs, **6** and **8**, of a seaside town, and a painting, **7**, of the same place. What made the artist paint it in this way? He was not interested in giving us a detailed picture of the town; he was only interested in its character. He liked this town very much and he looked hard to find what it was that made him like it, what it was that made this town so different from other seaside towns. He left out of his picture everything which was not important to him, and emphasised the pattern which gave the town its character.

6

7   **8**

The more character a thing has the easier it is to
recognise it. (Remember the rolls!) Sometimes we
find it useful to make a thing or a person easily
recognisable, as for instance in cartoons. To
understand cartoons, especially political cartoons, we
must be able to recognise easily everything and
everybody in them, and in order to make this possible
the artist must exaggerate character. This is called
caricature. Compare these photographs of politicians,
1, 2, 4 and **5**, with their caricatures, **3**. In what way

1

2 **3**

4

5

have their characteristics been exaggerated? Caricatures
are an exaggeration of character, but not a distortion.
Distortions are not more recognisable, but less so. If
you look at yourself in a distorting mirror, you may
find it hard to recognise yourself.

TO SUM UP

We say that something or somebody has character
when we notice a variation from the average.
Everything has character. The greater the variation
from the average the more pronounced the character.
We leave the mark of our character on everything we
do or make. If the character of a thing or person is
exaggerated it becomes a caricature. There is a
difference between exaggeration and distortion.

EXERCISES

1. Here are three drawings, **6**, **7** and **8**. Which object
in each group has the most character? Which object
in each group would you find easiest to recognise?

6

7

8

2. Look again at the drawing you did for exercise **3** on
page 49. Does it really express the character of your
neighbourhood? Could you improve on it now and
give it more character? Show the character of Hanley
(**5** on page 70) in a similar drawing.

3. Make tracings of **9** and **10** but trace only those
parts which you think give them their characters. Do
you think that your tracings show up the character of
each subject better than the photographs? Why?

9 10

73

4. Make a tracing of the face in picture **1**, but trace only those parts which give the face its character. Then change your tracing slightly to emphasise the character. Describe the character of this man.

5. Picture **2** shows the famous monument of General Colleoni by Verrocchio. It is a great study of human character; both the expression of the face, **3**, and the posture of the body describe the General in a way which suggests that the sculptor thoroughly understood him. Can you describe his character from this picture?

2 3

6. We can recognise handwriting because it is characteristic. Some people can recognise an author from the style of a story or a novel. You may be able to recognise a cricketer from the way he makes his strokes even if you are too far away to see his face. Can you think of other ways in which people's characters may be revealed?

7. Interpret picture **4**.

4

8

Nature's patterns

We are surrounded by a bewildering number of natural patterns, patterns produced by nature herself without any contribution from man. All these have one thing in common: they are the result of nature's attempts to achieve her purposes in the most efficient way. Take the pattern of a leaf for example. The main vein which runs up the middle splits into a number of smaller veins, and they in turn into yet smaller ones. In this way the whole area of the leaf can be covered and the sap be carried to and from any part. This is a good, practical arrangement and one which is often copied by man.

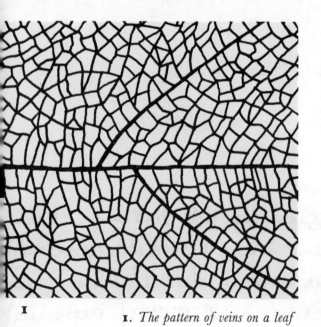

But this is not the only cause of the leaf pattern. What is the purpose of the leaf? It contains cells which catch sunlight needed by the plant for its food production. These cells must be able to absorb as much light as possible. To allow for this, the leaf spreads out as widely as it can. If the leaf were of uniform thickness, it could not spread far without becoming too heavy at its edges and tip. But leaves are constructed in such a way that they grow thinner and lighter towards their edges. The whole plant too gets thinner and lighter the higher it grows, so that the top of the main stem has less weight to carry than the lower part. If this were not so, the top of the plant might be too heavy and break the stem as it sways in the breeze.

As you see from these pictures, man-made patterns often have similar features to plant patterns. The reason for this is that they have similar problems to overcome.

1

1. The pattern of veins on a leaf

2. New Norcia Cathedral, Australia, and,
3, a model of its structure. Three leaf-like
patterns moulded into one huge structure

2
3

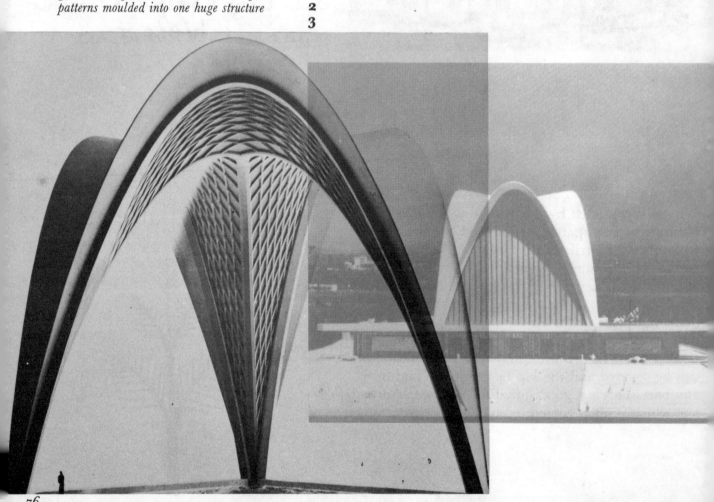

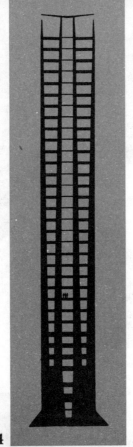

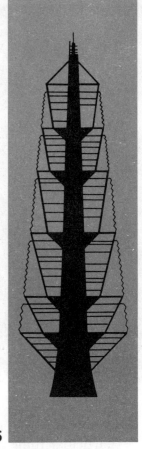

4

5

6

7

8

4. *The Pirelli building in Milan and,* **5,** *a drawing of its structure.* **6.** *A model of the exhibition tower, part of which you saw on page 23, and,* **7,** *a drawing showing how it is constructed.* **8.** *A water tower in Helsinki, Finland. What natural pattern does it remind you of?*

1   2

3

Nature does not reserve one kind of pattern for one particular thing. She does not hesitate to copy herself again and again if it suits her purpose, that is to say, when a certain pattern is required for practical reasons, and all natural patterns are highly practical. The principle is the same in all these leaf patterns, 2, even though they look different. The arrangement of leaves on a plant also varies, but here, too, the principle is always the same.

Nothing in nature stands still. There is constant movement in everything, but often the movement is so slow that we do not notice it. Patterns are changing all the time and the patterns we see around us are the outcome of a long process of change. Look at picture 3 of part of a sea shell called nautilus. Its pattern shows how it grows. Each time it adds another chamber to its house, it makes it a bit larger than the previous one, and in the end all the chambers link up into a pattern like the one in the picture. As in the case of the leaf, there are many different ways of applying this principle and some other examples are shown in pictures 4, 5, 6 and 7.

3. *A sea shell called nautilus.* 4, 5. *Minute fossilised shells, enlarged many times.* 6, 7. *Sea shells. All these are variations on the spiral construction.*

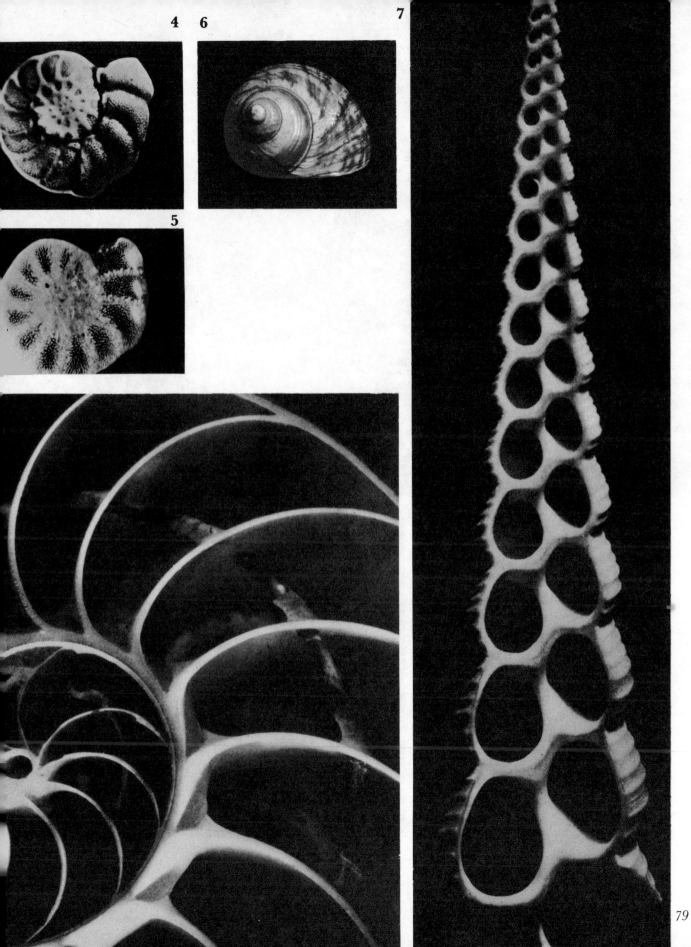

4 6 7

5

1. *The Colorado River and its tributaries*
2. *Trees against the sky*

*Pattern **3** was produced by an electrical discharge inside a block of plastic. It is a permanent record of the path of the discharge.*

4

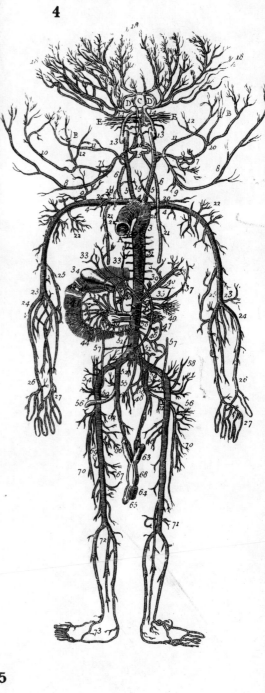

The tree pattern occurs frequently in nature. In the human body, **4**, it is repeated over and over again. An electrical discharge can be shown to have the same pattern, **3**. Even a chart of the evolution of life, **5**, takes the shape of a tree. Much of the living world appears to be organised in this pattern.

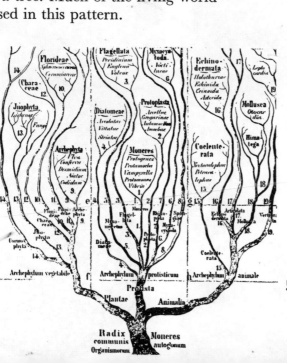

5

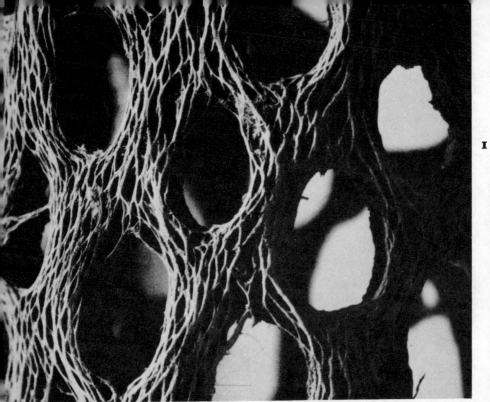

1. *The structural pattern of the cholla cactus and* **2,** *of wood.* **3.** *The Giants' Causeway, in Ireland,* **4,** *a wasps' nest, and* **5,** *a kind of radiolaria, a very small creature. We often find the same patterns on very small and very large objects.*

1 **2**

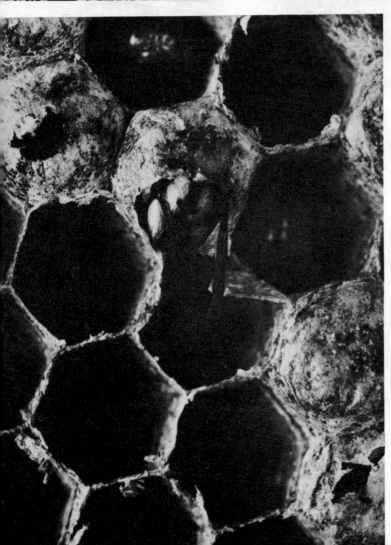

3

4 **5**

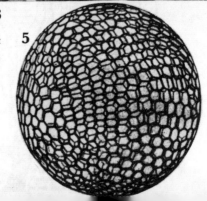

Remembering that nature's purposes are always practical, to understand nature's patterns we must first try and understand what caused them. Only then will they make sense to us. We do not fully understand the leaf until we have realised how it stretches itself out, thrusting its cells towards the light. The nautilus shell will mean much more to us when we understand that it grows in a spiral, getting larger all the time. Artists of all periods have tried to understand the patterns of nature and have not been content merely to copy their appearance. Drawing **7** from the notebook of Leonardo da Vinci shows how hard he tried to understand the patterns of moving water under different conditions. The other drawing, **6**, shows that his attitude to all patterns was really the same. The pattern of folds in the old man's garments are not just copied. This drawing is an attempt to understand what brought the pattern about.

6   7

1

2

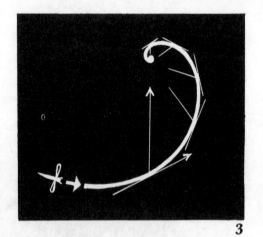

3 4

As well as being practical, all natural patterns have something else in common. They are all based on mathematical principles. You would expect a master builder to have definite ideas about the way he builds, and to use the same ideas in many different ways when it suited him. It is astonishing to think that all the patterns on this page, **1** to **7**, are based on a single principle which can be expressed in figures and formulae—even the pattern of the path of an insect approaching the light, **3**.

1. The spiral horns of Marco Polo's sheep and 2, a spiral staircase. 3. The path by which some insects approach the light. As the eyes are turned outwards the line of sight is not the same as the line of flight, shown by the two arrows. The combination of the two results in a spiral. 4. A pyrethrum, 5, a pine cone, 6, the tendrils of a passion flower, and 7, a spiral galaxy, have one thing in common – their spiral construction.

5   6
7

Nature builds her lovely patterns only for practical
reasons. We find similar patterns throughout nature.
Natural patterns are based on mathematical principles.

EXERCISES

1. Collect a few objects showing similar patterns,
draw them and explain why you think the same
pattern occurs in each of them.
2. Find a number of man-made patterns which are
similar to natural patterns. Try to explain this
similarity.
3. The organ in the Royal Festival Hall, **2**, is
completely open and you can see all the pipes. Do you
like this as a pattern? How did it come about? Is it
entirely man-made, or could it be called a partly
natural pattern?
4. Compare the two spirals, **1**. Which do you prefer
as a pattern? Why?
5. Look again at the pages from Leonardo's notebook.
Would you call him an artist or a scientist?
6. Look again at the family of patterns on page 79.
Some of them belong to animals which lived millions
of years ago; others are still in existence. What does
this indicate?

I

2

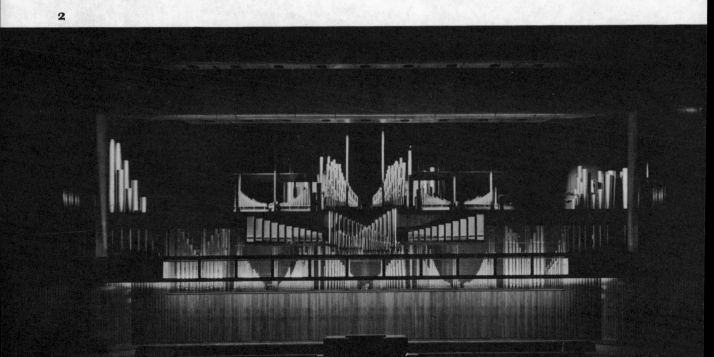

9

Solid patterns and light

Imagine you are on holiday at the seaside and you notice an artist in a deckchair, sketching. You look around you to see what it could possibly be that an artist would want to draw, but you see nothing interesting, just a few people playing about or basking in the sun—very ordinary indeed. Out of curiosity you stroll across and look over the artist's shoulder. You see a drawing something like **1**. You are surprised that there should be so many interesting patterns in a scene which had seemed so ordinary to you. You compare the drawing with what you can see; the artist has not invented anything: everything in the drawing really exists in the scene in front of you. With his highly trained eye the artist saw a pattern where you did not, but it was there all the time. There is the pattern of the deck chairs, most of them facing the same way, but some of them slightly out of line, which creates a pleasant contrast. Then there is the pattern of the legs, heads, deck chairs, clothes and towels, all adding up to one overall pattern which, now that you notice it, seems very pleasant. You would like to make a drawing of this scene, as the artist is doing, but you don't think you would make such a good job of it, so you run back to your beach bag, pull out your camera and return to the spot where the artist is sitting. You want your picture to be exactly the same as the artist's drawing so you take your snapshot from close to his head. When your holiday is over and you have had your film developed and printed, you look eagerly for this particular snapshot. but when you find it you are very much disappointed. Your snapshot looks something like picture **2**. The lovely pattern that you saw in the artist's drawing cannot be clearly seen, although your photograph and the artist's drawing show exactly the same scene. What has happened?

Compare the drawing and the photograph very carefully. The objects and people in both are the same, but they give a different impression. Why?

If you made a tracing of the drawing and put it on top of the photograph, you would find that everything corresponds except the amount of shadow inside all the shapes. This is the only real difference between the two pictures. But from this follows a further

1

2

difference. In the drawing the pattern is very strong: if you stood the photograph and the drawing side by side and looked at them from a distance, you would recognise the scene in the drawing long before you could make out the photograph. In the photograph the pattern is less marked but we can see much more clearly what each shape is like. The pattern you saw in the drawing does not stand out in the photograph because in the latter each object is broken up into smaller areas, black, white and grey, which make patches of light and shade. But although the pattern which the artist brought out is less prominent another pattern has emerged. If you look carefully you will see that the patches of light and dark also have a pattern about them. This new pattern is more difficult to see, but picture 3 will help us. This photograph was made from the same film as picture 2. But in order to make it easier for you to see the pattern of light and shade the photographer has printed it differently. He has got rid of all the greys; the lighter greys have turned into white, the darker ones have joined up with the blacks, so that only black and white are left. Now you can see the pattern of light and shade much more clearly. The photographer has not changed the pattern in the first photograph, but made it simpler, just as we can simplify a long story by leaving out the parts which are not essential to the plot.

2

If you now compare the artist's drawing with picture 3, you can see what the real difference is. In the drawing, the objects themselves—the deck chairs, the heads, the legs—make the pattern. In the photograph the pale and dark parts make the pattern, a pattern of light and shade. You can see that in some places the light part of one object merges with the light part of another and there is nothing to show exactly where each object ends. The objects themselves don't really come into this pattern, only the light and shade. Neither the kind of pattern an artist makes, nor a photograph can, by itself, tell us everything about a certain scene, or situation, or landscape. The one tells us about the way the shapes of the objects fit together, the other tells us about the light and shade, which in turn tell us something about the form of the objects.

3

We need both patterns to get a complete picture, and this is where your snapshot comes in once again. For in this photograph, now that we have thought about it carefully, you should have no difficulty in finding both patterns together, one on top of the other. The blending of both kinds of pattern is needed for a complete picture. This capital, 4, like your snapshot, contains two patterns. One is the pattern of the leaves and the other is the pattern of light and shade. The drawing 5, shows what the leaf pattern might have looked like if it had been done on a flat surface and not carved into the stone. The flat pattern is the same colour throughout, but in the carving the leaves sometimes catch the light, and sometimes curve back into the shadow. The spaces between the leaves are hollowed out and appear dark and mysterious. Some of the leaves cast a shadow onto their neighbours. By comparing the drawing with the photograph of the carving you will see that the artist who made the capital added a great deal to the pattern by giving it light and shade. It is so much more interesting than the simple flat pattern; it is fuller and richer.

A pattern in relief has one great advantage over flat patterns: as the light changes so the pattern changes. Every time you look at it, it will be a little different. This capital is not just one, or even two patterns, it is at least a thousand patterns. The mason who made it was very skilful, because the changing pattern of light and shade does not interfere with the pattern of the leaves. The two patterns work together and help each other. Neither would be so interesting without the other. The pattern of light and shade did not just happen. The mason thought about it as much as he thought about the pattern of the leaves; the two belonged together in his mind. He chose the position and angle of each leaf so that it should give the right kind of light and shade, which would then add up to the kind of pattern he wanted. That is why it is so successful. No matter from which angle the light happens to come, or from which side you look at it, this capital will always look right.

4

5

1

Here are some more examples showing patterns of light and shade. Each one of these is really two patterns in one. You can see that the light, as it strikes the pattern of shapes, adds something to it. In all these patterns the effect of the light was considered as the pattern was made. The patches of light and dark did not come about by accident. Designers are not always clever enough to understand the effect of the light, or else they have not the skill to put their knowledge to good use. The light then becomes an enemy instead of a friend and destroys the pattern. These letters, **3**, were cut in stone by Roman masons many hundreds of years ago. Each stroke is cut in the shape of a V-shaped trough and finished with a triangle. This is the best way of cutting letters in stone so that they are easy to read. Wherever the light comes from it will always be caught by some

3

*The pattern of light and shade is as important to films as it is to architecture. The right kind of lighting will help an actor's performance; for instance, it can stress the feelings he is trying to express. In what way does the lighting help in picture **2**?*

*The studded pattern in picture **4** goes right round the house. Light playing on it in different ways gives us many variations.*

2

part of the letter, while the other side of the stroke will appear dark because it is facing away from the light.

The Roman masons who invented these letters were certainly thinking of the light, just as the masons of the Southwell oak leaves were.

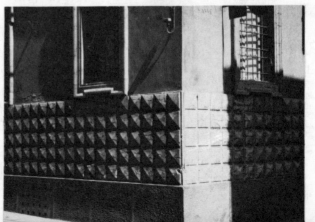

4

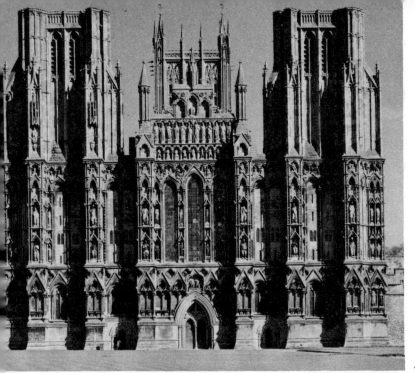

5   6

7

5. *Wells Cathedral*. **6**. *The Great Seal of England, 1651, showing the House of Commons*. **7**. *A Greek temple*. **8**. *Pottery tiles. This pattern consists of only two different types of tiles, a concave and a convex one. By arranging them in different ways many patterns can be made because the light takes part in the pattern making. The designers of all these patterns calculated the effect of the light on their patterns.*

8

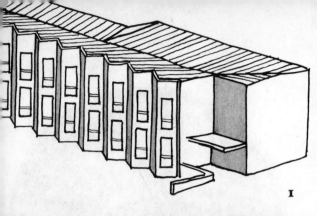

1

2

2. *Student accommodation in Karachi, Pakistan. Built imaginatively with standardised parts, it is positioned to catch the sea breeze.*

Light and shade are very important in all man-made patterns which contain *three-dimensional* forms. You already know that houses make patterns. Sometimes the pattern, as in the picture on page 50, is very dull and inhuman. Compare it with this Swedish building, **1**, and then with the Pakistani one, **2**. The architects who designed the buildings on this page have broken up what might have been depressingly flat fronts by allowing for interesting patterns of light and shade. But they have done more than that. The Swedish building, **1**, is so arranged that it makes the most of the view. The architect of building **2** has tried to keep out as much sun as possible and that is why the windows are so deeply set into the front of the house. The patterns of light and shade certainly help to enrich the fronts of these houses, but they spring naturally from the architects' practical purposes.

TO SUM UP
Three-dimensional forms always have a pattern of light and shade as well as a pattern of flat shapes. When the two patterns are designed to blend together, the resulting unified pattern can be much richer than a flat pattern.

EXERCISES
1. Examine picture **3**. This is a reproduction of a painting by Rembrandt, called 'The Woman taken in Adultery'. Take a piece of tracing paper and trace the flat pattern, that is to say the pattern of flat shapes. Then take another piece of tracing paper and trace the pattern of light and shade. Compare your tracings with the picture. Do you think that in the picture the two patterns are cleverly put together? Do they help each other or do they conflict? Give your reasons. What did Rembrandt achieve by arranging the patterns in this particular way?
2. Find two or three patterns which change with the light. Make rough sketches to show how they change and describe them.
3. Describe how the pattern of light and shade fits in with the overall patterns of buildings **4** and **5**.

Experiencing form through sight and touch

In the last chapter we have been looking at many different patterns: some were made up of flat shapes, the kind of pattern that can be used on papers and fabrics. Others contained solid shapes, such as the pattern of leaves in Southwell Minster. A flat shape on a fabric is no different in thickness from the rest of the fabric. If we touched it without looking at it we should not know it was there. But pass even one finger along a row of apples and you can feel the pattern even if you happen to be looking at something else. The pattern of the apples is composed of solid shapes or three-dimensional shapes. We call these solid shapes *forms* or even *solid forms*. Everything, from a pinhead to a mountain, that has length, breadth and thickness is a form.

The first important difference between a flat shape and a solid form is that the solid form may be touched and felt. The way to find out about a flat shape is to look at it. But there are other ways of finding out about a solid form. It has different faces which must all be looked at and touched if we wish to know and understand the whole form. If you hold a cricket ball in your hand without looking at it your sense of touch will tell you that it is a spherical object; but could you be sure that it is spherical by looking at it? Could

I

it not have a large bulge or dent at the back? You could be looking at half a cricket ball. You cannot be quite sure that it is spherical until you have closed your fingers round it and felt it. Although you can discover that it is spherical by walking all round it, your sense of its solidity will be much greater if you can also touch it. A form will have much more meaning for us if we can *experience* it through touch as well as sight.

Our sense of touch is not confined to our fingers. We can experience form with our whole bodies. These children are playing in an old hollow tree-trunk. When they first started to play there the old tree must have seemed rather strange to them, but as they played there, day after day, they got to know it better. First they learnt how to climb up on the inside of the trunk and then to sit on the top. On the way up they could look out through the holes left by branches which had broken off. Then they learnt how to balance on and hang from the two strong branches which still remained. In the end one child found he could get to the top from the outside. In order to do all these things the children had to find out as much as possible about the form of the old tree. They discovered supports for their feet, they found out where to hold on with their hands, where the surface was smooth and slippery, and so on. They know every square inch of the tree-trunk, both inside and out. A stranger comes along, walks round the tree and looks at it from all sides because it is a lovely shape, feels its trunk with his hand, and finally looks inside it. Do you think this person knows as much about the form of the tree-trunk as the children do? No matter how long he spends merely looking at it, or touching it with his hand, will he ever know as much about it as the children, who have experienced it with their whole bodies?

2

3. *This photograph has been taken by a camera which can see and record a complete form by 'looking all round it'. Such a camera can be said to experience form. Do you think this photograph tells us more than a front view would?*

3

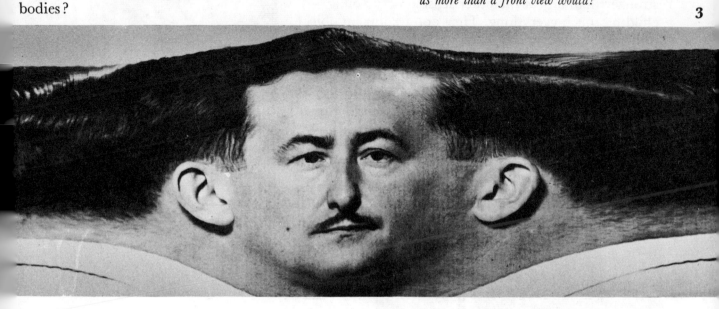

I

Of course there are forms which are too large to feel even with one's whole body, but they also can be experienced. Have you ever visited a cave and sensed the dank walls all round you although you could not see them? Did you hear the eerie echo of your own footsteps? Did you smell and breathe the cool, damp air? If you have ever done this you will know that by walking about inside the cave you experienced it through all five senses.

When we are very young our sense of touch is much stronger than any of the other senses. Very young children touch everything. They don't know an object until they have touched it. As we grow older and our senses and our minds develop, we easily get out of the habit of touching things. People who neglect their sense of touch are unable to experience form to the full. They may look at forms like the ones in pictures **3** to **5**, but they cannot take them in fully because they cannot experience them. They cannot make any real contact with them.

So far in this chapter we have dealt only with experiencing forms already in existence, but what happens when a form is made? Let us consider the potter as he *creates* a vessel. (Look up the word *create* in a dictionary.) He probably has a good idea in his mind of what he is going to do before he starts, but as he watches his vessel grow on the potter's wheel, he also feels with his hands the form he is creating. Eyes and hands work together in a complete partnership. We can think of it as a partnership of two friends working on the same job. Sometimes one of them will have a good idea, sometimes it will be the other who suggests the best plans. Together they produce something of which they can both be proud. The partnership is a subtle one, and it is not surprising that there are few people capable of creating satisfying forms.

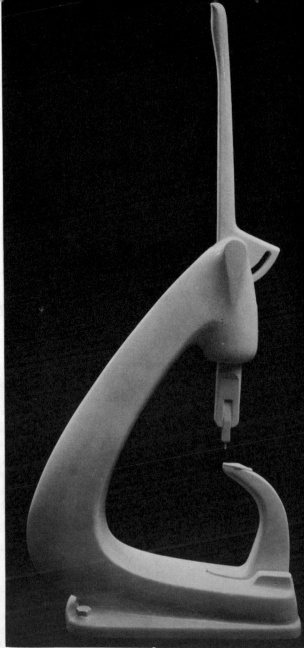

3

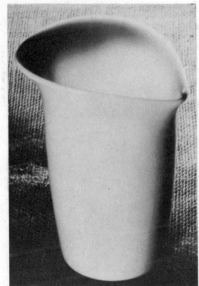

...pes like the jug, 3, the model ...ting machine, 4, and the pottery ...king fountain, 5, must have been ...erienced as forms by their designers.

5

Look at this door handle, **1**. It is quite well made, of a good material, and someone probably spent quite a long time designing it. We see so many door handles like this that we have come to accept their appearance. But how many of us ever stop to wonder whether this handle is a good shape? Not many people bother about the shape of door handles. But why not? Why should not the most ordinary object be well designed? Even the smallest detail of everything we make should be considered seriously. The door handle in picture **1** looks as though nobody ever thought about the way it would fit the hands of people using it. But what about this other door handle, **2, 3**? Its form is pleasant from any angle. The designer himself made the original

1

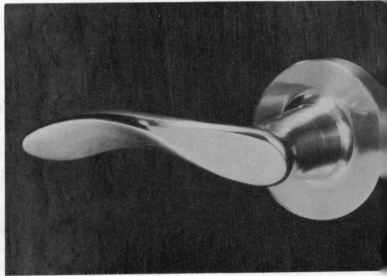

2 **3**

one with his own hands. He probably worked just like the potter, looking and feeling—experiencing—all the time until he was satisfied with the form of his handle. If you had one of these handles in front of you (perhaps you have a similar one at home) and gripped it, you would realise that it not only looks pleasant but also feels pleasant. It fits the hand better and is easier to grip and press down than the straight one. Because it pleases both our sense of sight and our sense of touch, and is easy to use, it is a good form.

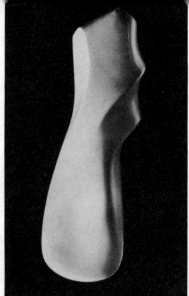

4   **5**   **6**

7

Here are some more handles, **4** to **7**, belonging to different kinds of tools, which have been experienced as forms by their designers. They are all different because the tools are for different jobs, and the handles have to be held in different ways. But they have all been shaped by the designers' own hands and eyes, just as the door handle, **2**, was. If you saw one of these tools lying on a table would you not want to pick it up? Good forms draw us towards them.

Handles are very special kinds of forms because they have to be gripped all the time the tool is in use, but what we have said about them also applies to other forms. The back of a chair is meant to support one's back. Look at the chair, **4**, on page 110. It seems to be a good and interesting form but you cannot judge it properly until you have sat in it and felt how it does its job.

8

10   **11**   **9**

*The earlier form of this electric razor, **8**, was not by any means the best possible form for such an implement, but the second version, **9**, is even worse. It has awkward corners and ornaments and does not fit the hand well. The connection for the wire tends to get in the way. It is a clumsy-looking form.*

*An old-fashioned tap, **10**, and a modern one, **11**. This surely is a change for the better. The modern tap is mechanically improved and more pleasant to handle and to look at.*

1 2
3

*The designers of this vertical press, **2 – 3**, made a very good job of it. It is not only better looking than the old one, **1**, but it is also more efficient.*

TO SUM UP

Everything that has length, breadth and thickness is called a form or solid form. Our own bodies are solid forms. In order to understand a solid form we must experience it, that is to say we must look at it from all sides, if possible touch it, and use as many of our senses as we can to understand it. Not many people try to experience solid forms in this way. Good designers make things which we can experience as satisfactory forms.

EXERCISES

1. On page 95 you saw children playing in a hollow tree trunk. Not all children have such a lovely toy. Picture **4** shows children playing in what we may call an abstract tree trunk. It does not really look like a tree nor is it meant to deceive the children into thinking that it is. But there is a similarity between the hollow tree and this big toy, **4**, which is made of concrete. What is it they have in common? If you could choose, which of the two would you rather play on? What are the advantages and disadvantages of both?

2. If the new razor in picture **9** on page 99 is not an improvement on the older kind, **8**, why do you think it was designed like this? Do you think its designer experienced it as a form?

3. Find some objects which have been redesigned like the press opposite. Compare the earlier with the later form. Do you think they have been improved? Give your reasons.

4. On page 99 you saw a number of well-shaped handles, **4** to **7**, but you did not see the tools they belonged to. At the bottom of this page you can see all the tools, **5** to **8**, but this time without their handles. Can you tell which handle belongs to which tool? Remember that each handle was designed for a certain tool, to be used in a particular way, and will fit only that one.

4

5   **6**   **7**   **8**

11

Seeing all round

It is quite easy to get to know the shape of a cricket ball but what about really irregular shapes? If you look at the surface of a flint you will notice many bumps and hollows. These little forms merge with one another and çannot be separated; altogether they make up the form of the whole flint. As you turn it between your fingers and examine each bump or hollow, you can see each of these little forms merging into another. The form seems to be flowing round the flint in a continuous movement.

How would you describe this flint in words? You could say that it has a number of bumps and points and will stand on its base. But there must be millions of flints which would answer to this description. You want to describe what gives this flint its particular character, and you soon realise that words are inadequate. Form moves and flows, and the only really satisfactory way of describing movement is by means of a cinema film. A single photograph cannot give us a very clear idea of a footballer scoring a goal or a dancer making a graceful turn, but a series of photographs can. The flowing form of the flint cannot be described properly by any other means. To print here a film of our flint in all its forms would take up more space than we can spare, so we shall look at only a few photographs showing the flint from different

angles. There are eight pictures covering the whole
surface and the ninth picture brings us back to our
starting point. There are many gaps in this series of
pictures, for much can happen to the form between one
picture and the next, but in spite of that, if you look
at these pictures one after the other, you may be able
to get an idea of the flow of the form. Slowly the
complete shape of the flint unfolds itself. We must
never forget that the form flows round an object. We
cannot possibly learn much about the form of a tree or
a house by looking at these objects from one side only.
It is like watching a dancer for only one second of a
long dance.

*Any one of these pictures of a dog
shows that it is moving, but by looking
at them all together we get a much
stronger impression of the character of
the movement.*

In picture **1** the solid arrow shows the direction of the movement in our film. But the form flows in all directions. Let us now watch the movement of the form in the direction shown by the dotted arrow. Here it is in the second film strip, **2**. Some of the forms are familiar, others are quite new. The flint is a solid form and to get to know it we must look at it from many different angles. Even a simple object, like a flint, has quite a complicated form.

I

2 **3**

If we were to arrange all our flint pictures on the table we should find that they add up to a pattern. If you think about it for a moment you will realise why. They are different views of the same form, and so they have something in common. We can simplify them and treat them as flat shapes, **3**. You can see that each one has a different outline, but they all belong to the same family. Looking at these shapes you know at once that they are related, even without seeing their common ancestor, the flint.

You have probably heard the word *harmony*. Harmony means agreement. When certain notes are played at the same time they give us a pleasant feeling because they agree—they fit well together. But harmony does not apply to music only. When certain shapes, such as the ones above, are grouped together they too give us a pleasant feeling because they are related to one another. We can say that these shapes harmonise.

What is happening in our minds as we look at different views of a solid shape? As we follow the flow of the form round the flint some of the many different shapes are retained as patterns in our minds. What you later remember of the flint is a pattern like picture **3**. When the pattern is harmonious, as this one is, the memory is a pleasant one. All the different aspects of any natural form are in harmony. That is why we enjoy looking at natural shapes.

This magnificent sea shell, 4, has a more complicated shape than the flint, but whichever way you look at it you will always see shapes which are related to each other and which harmonise.
These shapes easily fall into a pattern.

4

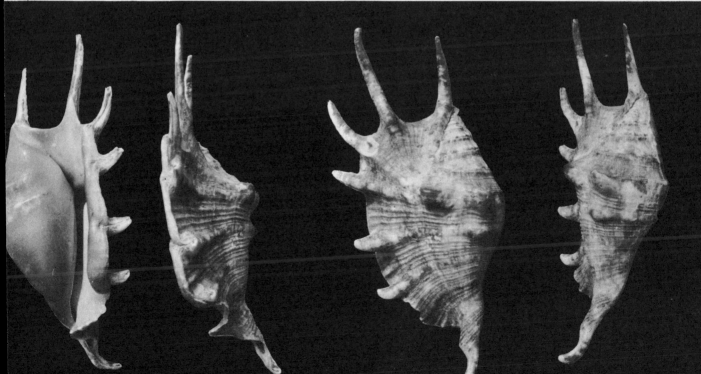

1

The different views of this piece of drift-wood have a harmonious family resemblance.

A combination of all the impressions we receive of any natural object gives us a feeling of a harmonious whole, and if man-made objects are to give us as much pleasure as natural ones, we must be able to sense in them a pattern of related and harmonious shapes. The designer who experiences the object he is making, sensing how the form flows round it, will produce shapes as good as natural ones. As you look at this glass dish, **2**, from many different angles your impression of it will grow deeper and richer because the pattern of forms is harmonious and pleasant. Such an object will continually give us pleasure because every time we look at it another facet of its character is revealed. It is easy to feel a kind of friendship for it.

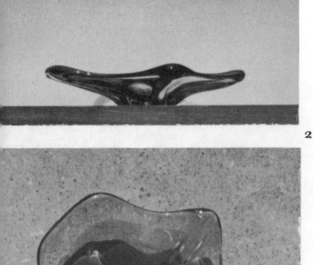

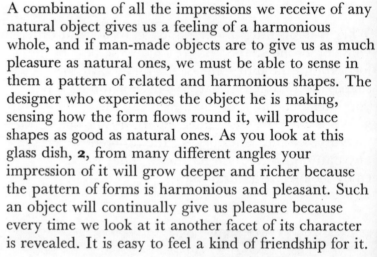

2   **3**

3, 4, 5. *Different views of a sculpture by Henry Moore*

4

5

Buildings too should be experienced as forms. One view of a great cathedral is only part of the whole story. Pictures **1** to **3** show how it looks from several different angles. All these views together give an impression of the whole building as one vast form and the continuous pattern of the decorations helps to relate the different views. If you could walk round the cathedral you would experience the unbroken form.

2

1 **3**

A great building like Ely Cathedral looks right from every angle, even from above.

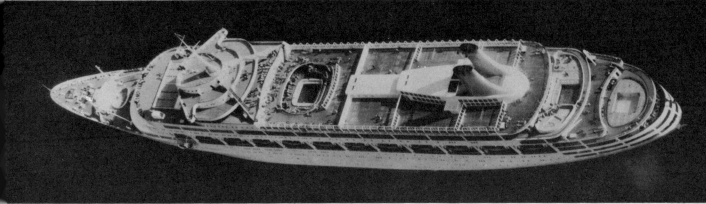

4

5

The 'Canberra' is a perfectly designed form both inside and out. The wonderful shape of the outer case, 4 and 5, is well matched by the interior design, for example the staircase, 6.

6

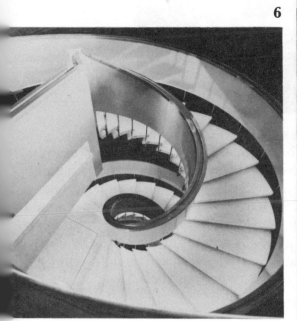

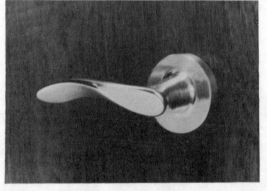

Many man-made shapes do not give this impression of unity and harmony. Here are two views of a house, **1**, **2**. You may like the front, **2**, but of course the front is only part of the whole form. If you walk round the house to look at it from other angles, you come to this back view, **1**. Not only is this very unpleasant in itself but it does not fit in with the front or any other part of the house. There is no pattern of related and harmonious shapes. When nature creates she does not put all the pleasant things at the front and all the unpleasant ones at the back, hoping that nobody will look there. We must take care that the things we make harmonise with their natural surroundings and with

each other. This is the way of ensuring that they harmonise with us. Some of the modern buildings you have seen in this book show that it is possible to build whole and complete forms. The door handle, **5**, and the chair, **4**, were made with the same care and would fit in with such a building, **3**, quite easily. But the house, **1**, **2**, with the pretty front and the ugly back, will never look right because its designer never thought of it or experienced it as a harmonious whole.

Picture **6** shows the monument to Giuliano dé Medici in Florence. It is the work of Michelangelo, one of the greatest Italian sculptors. The central figure is placed in a niche and can therefore only be seen from the front. Probably the back of the statue had never been seen by anyone but Michelangelo and his assistants. You might think that he would not have bothered to finish off the back properly, knowing that it would never be seen. During the war the sculpture was taken down to be stowed away in safety and for the first time since it was installed the back could be seen. Photograph **7**, which was taken at the time, shows that the back, although not polished, is as complete as the front. All the forms and ornaments, even quite minor ones, are fully realised. In order to make such a great piece of sculpture Michelangelo had to experience the complete form. If he had not bothered about the back the pattern of shapes in his mind would have been disturbed and inharmonious.

Form is a continuous movement. If we look at natural forms from different angles, we see that they are composed of related shapes which make up a harmonious whole and which consequently create a harmonious pattern in our minds. We find such forms satisfying. We must take care that the forms of man-made objects create harmonious patterns too. If the pattern is inharmonious the form will not satisfy us. Satisfying forms can be created only by designers who experience the objects they make as unified wholes.

EXERCISES
1. Take a natural object, such as a flower, or a sea shell, or a twig. Turn it slowly in your hands and look carefully at all its different shapes. Pick out three or four of these, the ones you like the best, and sketch them. Try and arrange the shapes in a pattern.
2. Do the same with various man-made objects. Decide which has the most successful form.
3. On page 106 we said it was easy to feel a kind of friendship for a harmonious form. Do you think this is true? Is it easier to feel friendly towards the chair, **4**, on page 110 than towards an object like the house, **1, 2**, on the same page?
4. What do you think we mean when we say that the things we create should be in harmony with us?

1

The patterns and forms we need

12

To experience a form fully we must try and understand its character as a whole, and that includes the material it is made of and its surface. If you look again at Henry Moore's sculpture on page 107 you will see what an important part of the character of the form lies in the material. The sculptor selected the stone in order to achieve exactly this effect. Without this particular surface our experience of the form would be different. This is not surprising because every kind of surface has a character of its own. When we look at the flat surfaces in picture **1**, each one of them

makes a different impression on us, because it is made
of a different material or of the same material treated
differently. If we imagine various surfaces applied to
the same three-dimensional form we realise that the
form must be influenced by the character of each
surface, its texture, colour and pattern. Look at the
two pictures of the chair. From picture **2** we
appreciate the chair's form and clever construction
and the efficiency with which it does its job, but that
is not all that we need to know about it. Picture **3**
shows the texture of the chair, and from this we can
understand that the designer thought of this chair and
experienced it as a wooden form. In considering any
object we must bear its surface in mind.
Looking at the gleaming metal surfaces of many of our
industrial forms, **4**, the rough surfaces of reinforced

4

concrete architecture, **2**, the sleekness of plastic objects, **1**, the knobbly surface of a tree trunk, **3**, the unique weathered quality of an old stone sculpture, **4**, we can readily understand that the surface of any form is an important element in its character. If we were to copy any object in a different material and place it next to the original we should be faced by two forms whose character and appearance differed greatly.

1 2

3

4

114

5   6

An object has value and meaning only through its
relation to other things. Relationships are of the
greatest importance in our understanding of both
natural and man-made objects. You already understand
enough about form and pattern to know why the
pattern of birds, **5**, is so harmonious and the reason
for the happy relationships between the different
shapes in this picture. But there are many more kinds
of relationships. A bouncing ball assumes many
different forms, **6**, but we can feel a relationship
between them for they all come from the same basic
form.

The play of light on these forms, **7**,
*creates shapes and patterns which
are related,* **8**.

7

8

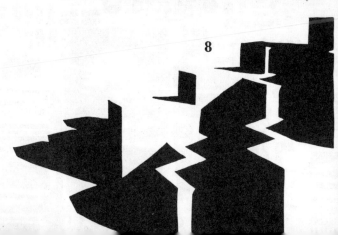

If two patterns, **2** and **3**, are combined, as shown in picture **4**, the resultant new pattern, **5**, will include features of the character of both original patterns—as children show characteristics of both parents. The new pattern is related to each of the original patterns. The individual shapes of the new pattern are related to each other because of their shared relationship to the original patterns.

Parts which belong to the same mechanism and work together also have a relationship with each other and so form a pattern like picture **1**, which shows the different parts belonging to the same typewriter.

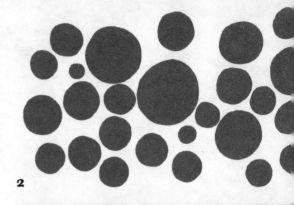

2

1

3

4

5

*If you place **2** on top of **3**, as shown in picture **4**, and then trace only those parts which are common to both patterns, the result will be the pattern in picture **5**.*

6

Picture **6** shows the pieces left over after a natural shape, a leaf, has been cut out of a rectangle. Each shape combines the character of the rectangle with the character of the leaf; that is why they are related and make a pleasant pattern. A plant against a geometric background, **7**, also creates a pattern of related shapes. The world is full of such relationships. We can recognise many of them quite easily if we examine them with care, as we have examined the patterns on these two pages. The vast majority, however, are too remote or too subtle to be more than sensed. A pattern may be defined as a series of relationships. Although we are often unable to see the exact relationships which make up a pattern we are able to sense its presence.

7

This sculpture by Barbara Hepworth is really a three-dimensional pattern.

8

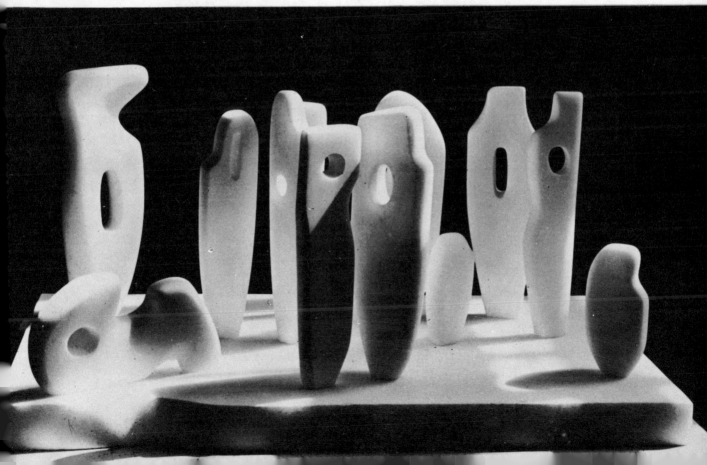

The architect of these buildings in Toronto, **1** and **2**, established a relationship between them; they certainly look as though they belong together. The sculpture in front of the President's Palace in Brasilia, **3**, is related to its background. The huge pattern of a town includes many different relationships which, as we grow familiar with them, form a pattern in our minds. As we saw from picture **6** on page 117, when such a pattern consists of related shapes it is a happy pattern. When the shapes are unrelated or identical they form a bad pattern which has a bad effect on us even though we may not be conscious of this.

1. 2. Two aspects of the Municipal buildings in Toronto, Canada

4, 5. Two views of the Market Square, Harlow New Town. Compare this with picture 3 on page 47. Do you think these three views add up to a harmonious pattern?

4   5

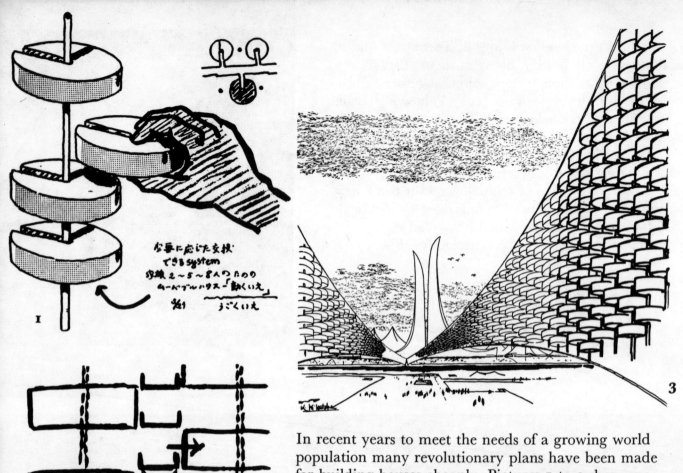

In recent years to meet the needs of a growing world population many revolutionary plans have been made for building houses cheaply. Pictures **1** to **3** show one such plan which seems both economical and adaptable, as new dwellings can be added when required, or removed when not needed any longer. But what about the overall pattern of a town built on this plan? Would you call it a human pattern? How is it likely to affect the people who live in the town? One of the dangers of our age is that we may use our great resources to build to a pattern not always in keeping with the true needs of human beings.

This house, **4**, is so designed that it has become part of its surroundings. It is partly built of the rock on which it stands and seems to have acquired its character. It blends so well with the natural pattern of its setting that it is difficult to imagine a time when it was not there. Yet it looks every inch a building of our century.

Although we cannot always achieve it, in making any object we must seek a similarly close relationship between materials and surroundings.

1 and 2 show how prefabricated dwellings may be arranged and put together. Further dwellings can be added, or taken away as the need arises. 3 shows a complete town built on this idea.

4
5

4. *The name of this house is Falling Water. It was designed by the American architect Frank Lloyd Wright.* **5.** *The Trevi Fountain in Rome. The sculptor of this fountain left part of the stone in its natural state. What do you think he tried to achieve by this?*

If you look at any natural shape or pattern you will appreciate that in nature's constructions material, function, and environment must be perfectly related, **1** to **4**. Man, being part of nature, seeks in his own creations to achieve this perfect relationship. Beautiful objects made by man in past ages show how skilfully he has used his materials to satisfy his needs. Today our problem remains the same—finding the ideal relationship between material, function and environment—but we cannot solve it by imitating the methods of earlier craftsmen. Like them we must be bold and ingenious in our planning, evolving our own methods to meet our own needs.

3

4

1. *Brain coral.* **2**. *Section through the stem of a plant.* **3**. *Uranus.* **4**. *Nautilus shell*

5

The baptistry at Parma, Tuscany, **5**, and the concrete canopy over the entrance to the UNESCO building, **6**. The patterns and shapes of the past should serve us as inspiration but we must not imitate them blindly. These two patterns are different in conception; each was designed for the materials and needs of its own times. In a similar way engineers have produced wonderful shapes and patterns, such as the turbine, **7**.

6

7

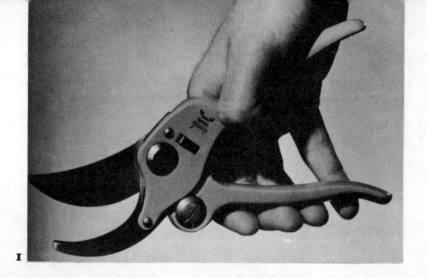

The pruner, **1**, the school, **2**, and the
airliner, **5**, are well designed; that is to
say, they are true to their materials, and
efficient and pleasant to use.

Above all we must remember that whatever we make
is for use by human beings, will be seen by human
beings, will influence them in many ways and will
shape their characters. We must learn to recognise
and select only those shapes and patterns which work
with and not against the laws of nature. If we fail to
do this we shall have lost the great opportunities which
our age has placed in our hands.

2

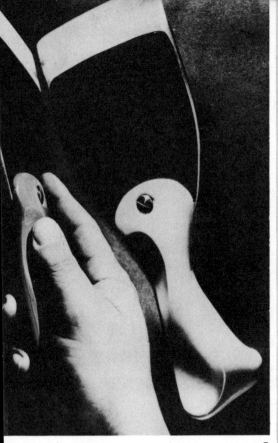

3

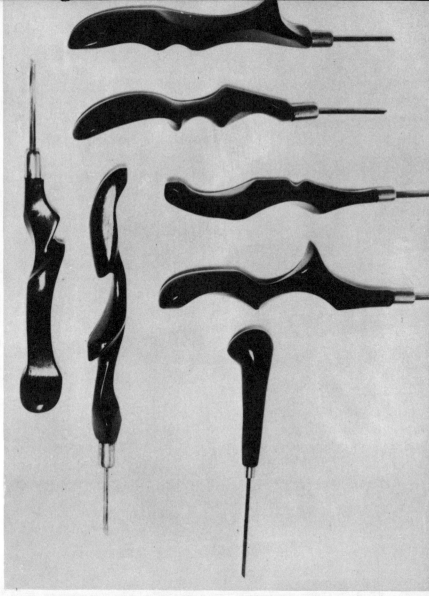

4

Modern materials make it possible for us to design more efficient shapes. In the past handles were usually made of wood and turned on a lathe. They had, therefore, to be round. But plastic handles, **3** and **4**, are moulded, and can be made into almost any shape desired to fit their purpose.

5

1 2

EXERCISES

1. Here are three pictures. Discuss each one and explain what led the artist to make it abstract.

'Bullfight', **1**, *and 'Weeping Woman'*, **2**, *both by Picasso. 'Deluge'*, **3**, *by Leonardo da Vinci*

3

2. Compare the external staircase of the UNESCO
building, **4**, with the metal staircase, **5**. Discuss their
shapes and their relationships with the buildings.

4

5

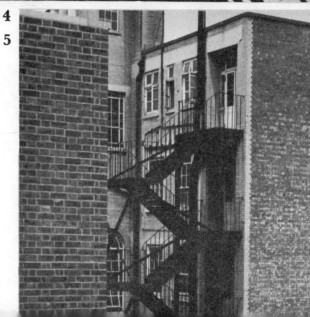

3. These baskets, **1, 2, 3,** were made at different times in different parts of the world, yet their patterns are similar. What accounts for this?

4. What is wrong with patterns **4** and **5**?

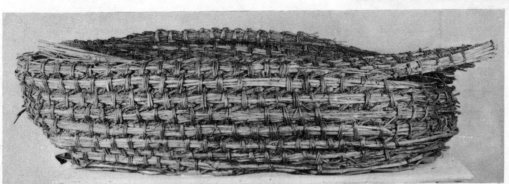

1. Basket from Sardinia. **2.** *Baskets from Sweden.* **3.** *Basket from ancient Egypt.*

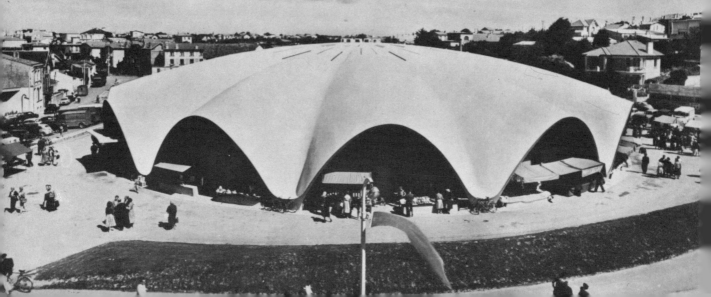